Living the
HIMpossible
Life

A collection of spiritual insights
compiled and edited by

BARRIE & HOLLY DOWN

malcolm down
PUBLISHING

23 22 21 20 19   7 6 5 4 3 2 1

First published 2019 by Malcolm Down Publishing Ltd.
www.malcolmdown.co.uk

British Library Cataloguing in Publication Data
A catalogue record for this book is available from the British Library.

ISBN 978-1-912863-22-8

Cover design by Fortunato Taddei

Printed in the UK

Only the eyes of your heart can look at
these things and know they are real.

(paraphrased from Eph. 1:18)

Contents

Acknowledgements   9

Foreword   11

CHAPTER 1 The IN HIM Life

1.1 The IN HIM life   20
1.2 Who are you?   21
1.3 Our blood covenant relationship   22
1.4 The basics of life IN HIM   24
1.5 Your place IN HIM   26
1.6 I put myself into you   28
1.7 The reality of the IN HIM life   30
1.8 MY strength, not yours   32
1.9 Treasures in earthen vessels   34
1.10 Living by the promptings   35

CHAPTER 2 Living This Impossible Life

2.1 Without ME you can't do it   38
2.2 Doing the impossible   39
2.3 It cannot be reasonable   41
2.4 This life is not what it looks like   42
2.5 I do it MY way   43
2.6 Having your being IN HIM   44
2.7 These are the days   46
2.8 HE's doing a new thing   48
2.9 This is who I AM and this is what life in the SPIRIT is   50

CHAPTER 3 Being Led

3.1 I am the good Shepherd   54
3.2 I will show you and you will go   55
3.3 Doors   56
3.4 Walking through the door   57
3.5 You have not chosen me but . . .   59
3.6 You thought you did it   61

CHAPTER 4 The Time is Now

4.1 The time is now   64

4.2 We walk in the expectation   65

4.3 Seeing things differently   66

4.4 The ice blocks are cracking   68

CHAPTER 5 Gifts and Callings

5.1 I made you, so I know you   72

5.2 This life under the radar   73

5.3 Life in the body   75

5.4 Demonstrating Jesus   76

CHAPTER 6 HIS Abundant Provision

6.1 Abundant life   80

6.2 Waves of supply   82

6.3 Overwhelming abundance   84

6.4 The doors to HIS provision   86

6.5 Managing lack   87

6.6 The supply and the tyranny of self   89

6.7 More than enough   91

CHAPTER 7 Life in the Spirit Realm

7.1 The sounds of the Spirit   94

7.2 The sound of the SPIRIT   95

7.3 The sound of "no limits"   96

7.4 Speaking from within   97

7.5 The IN HIM place   99

7.6 Cause and effect   100

7.7 Time and the two realms   102

7.8 The SPIRIT does not conform to the earthly   104

CHAPTER 8 Earthly Realm versus Spirit Realm

8.1 SPIRIT versus flesh   108

8.2 The work of the supernatural   110

8.3 Living our life down here   112

8.4 Freedom from encumbrances   114

8.5 HE is the GOD who changes things   115

8.6 The big lie of the flesh   116

8.7 Remember who you are   118
8.8 It's new every day   120

CHAPTER 9 Moving into the Spirit Realm
9.1 Moving from the natural to the supernatural   124
9.2 Stepping out   125
9.3 Deep wells   126
9.4 Music and Worship 1   128
9.5 Music and Worship 2   130
9.6 Receiving the things of GOD   131
9.7 Suddenly, everything changes   133
9.8 Praise – The Answer   135

CHAPTER 10 Seated Above in the Higher Place
10.1 The higher place   138
10.2 The place of joy and peace and supply   142
10.3 A life of above and beyond   144
10.4 Looking beyond   145
10.5 Moving a thought up higher   146

CHAPTER 11 Benefits of Life IN HIM
11.1 HIS extravagance   150
11.2 Complete provision   151
11.3 Authority   152
11.4 Ruling and reigning   154
11.5 Constant care   156
11.6 A new creation   157
11.7 YOU make the way   159
11.8 Living in the hidden place   161
11.9 Always working on your behalf   163
11.10 It's already done   165

CHAPTER 12 The Choice to Overcome Fear
12.1 The power of decision   168
12.2 Stepping out in HIM   170
12.3 The repercussions of trying to figure things out for yourself   171
12.4 No way out, except   172
12.5 There are no concerns   173
12.6 The fear of being wrong   174

CHAPTER 13 Stop It! Just Do It!

13.1 I never told you to do it yourself   176

13.2 I don't allow it   177

13.3 Why I shed my blood   178

13.4 So stop it   179

13.5 Expulsion   180

13.6 Let it go, it's just baggage   181

13.7 Just because you don't see it . . .   183

CHAPTER 14 The Power of Words

14.1 Your words and my life   186

14.2 Power of words   187

14.3 Stepping out on HIS words   189

14.4 You get to say what you want   190

14.5 Declare what you know to be true   191

CHAPTER 15 The Blood

15.1 The Blood never stops   194

15.2 The protection of the blood   196

15.3 Living the impossible life   197

15.4 The work of the Blood in the believer   199

15.5 New Covenant existence   202

Acknowledgements

We can take little credit for this book.

The words are the thoughts and inspirations of the Holy Spirit, expressed verbally and recorded as they were spoken, transcribed, sorted, and collected into chapters.

These spoken words were edited and put into their present format by Athena Taddei. To her goes the credit for making the words readable and understandable for you, the reader.

To Kerry Carmichael goes the credit for constant encouragement, expressed in so many different ways, to make these words into a book.

To Fortunato Taddei goes the credit for his creative input into cover design.

Finally, to our nephew Malcolm Down for offering to publish a book that does not follow the form of other books.

We are grateful and in awe of these friends, and trust that you, the reader, will receive what you need from the Originator.

Barrie & Holly Down

Foreword

[6]Yet we do speak wisdom among those *spiritually* mature [believers who have teachable hearts and a greater understanding]; but [it is a higher] wisdom not [the wisdom] of this present age nor of the rulers and leaders of this age, who are passing away; [7]but we speak God's wisdom in a mystery, the wisdom once hidden [from man, but now revealed to us by God, that wisdom] which God predestined before the ages to our glory [to lift us into the glory of His presence]. [8]None of the rulers of this age recognized *and* understood this *wisdom*; for if they had, they would not have crucified the Lord of glory; [9]but just as it is written [in Scripture],

"THINGS WHICH THE EYE HAS NOT SEEN AND THE EAR HAS NOT HEARD, AND WHICH HAVE NOT ENTERED THE HEART OF MAN, ALL THAT GOD HAS PREPARED FOR THOSE WHO LOVE HIM [who hold Him in affectionate reverence, who obey Him, and who gratefully recognize the benefits that He has bestowed]."

[10]For God has unveiled them and revealed them to us through the [Holy] Spirit; for the Spirit searches all things [diligently], even [sounding and measuring] the [profound] depths of God [the divine counsels and things far beyond human understanding]. [11]For what person knows the thoughts and motives of a man except the man's spirit within him? So also no one knows the thoughts of God except the Spirit of God. [12]Now we have received, not the spirit of the world, but the [Holy] Spirit who is from God, so that we may know and understand the [wonderful] things freely given to us by God. [13]We also speak of these things, not in words taught or supplied by human wisdom, but in those taught by the Spirit, combining and interpreting spiritual thoughts with spiritual words [for those being guided by the Holy Spirit]. (1 Cor. 2:6-13)

Introducing you to *The HIMpossible Life* and its authors is both a great honour, delight, and worthy challenge.

There are not many written works today where the authors have taken the words and thoughts of the mind of God given to them in "too many to count" times of prayer, meditation, and worship and set them in such a clear, simple, and wondrously delicious form. I was asked by Barrie and Holly to write this foreword because I am a witness to their history in Him for the past three decades, and in many ways have been a participant as well!

I have been a friend, prayer partner, traveller, and adventurer in God with Holly Down for thirty years at the time of this writing. She has been a great gift from above for all of this time. Holly's husband Barrie, in an act of pure bravery, began to gather with the two of us to pray and discuss the realms of God several years ago when his work schedule was altered and he had the days to fill.

At first it was unusual to have a man join our usually female-only times of prayer, worship, and consideration of the Scriptures, but I knew it was of the Lord and pressed on we did. Barrie's brilliant and articulate detailed mode of thought lifted us into new realms of understanding, and our emotive, female abandonment to prayer collectively brought the three of us to new realms in Him, our Beloved Saviour, Healer, Spirit, Redeemer, Giver of Gifts, the Lord Jesus the Anointed One.

One powerful truth that has risen up in our times together over the past several years is the knowing of the mystical, spiritual nature, and reality of the Body of Christ, both now in the earth and, at the same time, seated with Him in heaven. This dichotomy of living in two realms at the same time will be clearly seen in the writing of Barrie and Holly. These words from His very breath came from their spirits as they gazed upon Jesus both seated above and walking within each of them! We like to refer to it as "walking in our Jesus Life, as He walks in His Barrie, Holly, and Kerry life".

The challenge I have in writing this foreword is to maintain your focus on what follows and with that in mind, I will share one experience that Holly and I had in Scotland in 2010. I believe this experience will stand as an example of our HIMpossible life!

I had received word from a friend that there was a Prayer Tour planned in the fall of 2010 to the places of past revivals in Scotland. When I understood that we would visit the Isle of Lewis I knew immediately that I was to go on this trip. (My maternal grandparents were from Lewis and instrumental in praying me through my early years in the 1970s. The Lord had made me aware that it was their prayers that carried me through the darkness into His presence in 1972.) In planning this travel the Lord told me 'that Holly had to be on the trip' as well. Off we went to Glasgow in the fall. Arriving a day or two early to allow for jet lag, we stayed in a wonderful guest house just outside of Glasgow where we were to meet up with the tour. On the first night, seated at a table for two for dinner, I was taken up with an anointing of the Spirit and began to tell Holly about "my testimony", how the Lord had rescued me in 1972. Now, I was keenly aware that I had shared this story more than once with Holly, but I was almost incapable of stopping my story. I was watching myself tell her about the little housekeeping cottage I was living in at the time in Colwood, BC. I was saying to myself, "Kerry, what are you doing, Holly knows this story," but on I went. I repeated how I was sitting on my couch when a dark cloud entered the room and I began to have dark thoughts about my existence on the earth. I got to the thought of why I was actually living, when the Spirit within me (I was brought up in church and filled with the Spirit and spoke in tongues from the age of 11) shouted, 'Jesus, Jesus,' at which point I was very aware of warm oil pouring onto my head, trickling down my face, to the point of blurring my vision for at least 30 minutes and then proceeding over my whole body. I then found myself on the floor, in another room, prostrate before the Lord, weeping uncontrollably. As I became more aware I heard the voice of Jesus speaking to me: "Kerry, I love you and

I need you." In those moments my life was transformed and perhaps another book is ahead to speak of what followed, but back to Glasgow and Holly.

When I finished retelling my story, I believe I apologized to Holly for repeating myself, but we were both very aware of His presence. Holly then took up the revealing with questions of, "Where was that cottage exactly, and how big was it and what was it like?"

Holly, Barrie, and their children moved to Sooke, BC two years after I had my "meeting with the Holy Spirit". Their house was not ready for them so they rented a housekeeping cottage for several weeks until they could move into a permanent home.

On that evening in Glasgow, after two decades of friendship, on our travels to a week of walking in a revival anointing in Scotland with Pastors Karen and Paul Brady of Northern Ireland, Holly and I came to the realization of the fact that both of us had experienced supernatural visitations of the Lord, two years apart, in the same housekeeping cottage in Colwood, BC.

Holly had been brought up in an Anglican home, and at the age of five gave her heart to Jesus. She had always loved Jesus as a child and gone through the sacraments of communion and confirmation. She even shared her faith to her little school friends, and as she grew up she was always aware of Him at some level.

During the 1970s, with all of its upheaval, wars, riots, and overthrow of authorities in almost every domain, coming of age was confusing, frightening, and in many cases dangerous. There were new religions, drugs, the birth of feminism, and Eastern philosophies. For Holly, who met Barrie at a young age and married at 19, life was not without anxiety and fear. She was feeling lost and looking for a peace of heart and mind in 1974 when they had moved to British Columbia. Nothing seemed to fill the void in her spirit and thus we find Holly one night in this same housekeeping cottage, after Barrie and the children had gone to bed, sitting cross-legged on the floor in the living room, meditating on her inner flame, hoping to connect with a pool of peace and tranquility. In that moment, Holly became aware of a presence in the room and looked up to see Jesus standing before her. He didn't say anything to her but His very personage and presence greatly impacted Holly and this deepened her search to find the hope and peace that Jesus is! A few weeks after this experience Holly was awakened in the night to hear a voice say to her, "Peace be still!" She was aware that the Lord was calling and the next morning Holly, along with the children, visited a small Anglican mission church in the area. She doesn't remember a lot of what was said that morning, but she was keenly aware of five women who were in the congregation and involved in the service. As Holly tells it, "Every time I looked at those women who were busying themselves with serving and ushering, I saw lights that looked like fireflies just over their individual heads." When the service ended Holly approached them separately and told them each about being wakened in the night before. These women recognized the working of the Spirit and invited Holly to a prayer meeting they had together, with babysitting, one day during the week.

When the day arrived to attend the prayer meeting, Holly was anticipating this moment. When one of the ladies said, "Let's pray," Holly bowed her head as she was taught, and immediately became aware that Someone had entered the room. She opened one eye and saw no new visitor, except she knew, for the first time, that Jesus had entered the room!

At the end of the meeting, one of the ladies gave Holly a copy of a book by Merlin Carothers called Prison to Praise and shared about the power of praise and its ability to lift you up into the Spirit.

On another week, one of the ladies gave Holly a pamphlet about surrendering your life to Jesus. That night Holly read the words and talked to Jesus in a way she had never done before, surrendering her all to Him; He had to be real because she was at her wit's end! Her last words of prayer were, "Fill me with your Spirit," and she lifted her hands in praise and surrender when all of a sudden she began to sing an octave higher than normal and in a language she had never heard before! Holly finally knew that Jesus was and is real!

Barrie had been working late that night and when he came home Holly announced to him that "Jesus is real!" His reply was, "Have you been drinking?" Barrie was not yet ready to re-engage with a Saviour and an upbringing that he had hoped to leave far behind when he moved from England to Canada!

However, within a few weeks Barrie had watched the change in Holly and was aware that something spiritual had occurred in her life. He finally accepted the invitation to join Holly and the children one morning at church. Somewhere during the service, as Barrie struggled with the Holy Spirit's tugging on his spirit, his hands clutching the back of the pew in front of him, Barrie look down and saw the words "Try It Now" carved in the pew in front of him. There was no mistaking that Jesus was on his case, and Barrie's heart could no longer deny the inevitable result of responding to the wooing of the love of Jesus.

Within a short period of time Holly heard the Spirit say of Barrie, "Go back to your roots." Barrie's father was a Pentecostal minister in England and Barrie had been brought up by parents who lived by faith and walked in the Spirit. They connected with the local Pentecostal church and began attending under the leadership of Revd Don McMillan, who proved to be the one the Lord used to take them deeper in the life of the Spirit.

Within a year or so, Barrie and Holly were led to return to Toronto and shortly thereafter, found themselves in the Pentecostal Bible School in Peterborough, Ontario. Miracle after miracle followed them all these days. Provision, direction, divine connections were the order of day.

Both Barrie and Holly are filled with the Spirit, with the evidence of speaking in other tongues. This experience has engendered countless arguments, church splits, separations within the Body of Christ, and numerous books written throughout the history of the Body of Jesus Christ, however, it is through praying in the Spirit, by the Spirit, and of the Spirit that the words that follow have been inspired, interpreted, and written down for your enjoyment, enlightenment, and revelation of who you really are in Christ Jesus!

Their life together, which I have the privilege of sharing in on a regular basis, is a tonic of joy mixed with worship, dabbed by intense prayer, resulting in sounds and words from a deep place in Him. Words that flow from both of them, yet seem to be from one, filled with light and texture and a depth in God are the result of His call, His plan, and His purpose in them and through them to you! Don't be afraid to let go of the structure and bent what you think you know of Jesus and allow the life in the words that follow to open new places in the realms of God which were purchased by His blood for us to live in.

"Freely you have received, freely give!"

Kerry Carmichael

CHAPTER 1
The IN HIM Life

1.1 The IN HIM life

We are a unique creation.
We are a new creation, IN CHRIST.

We are HIS workmanship, created IN CHRIST JESUS.
We are bought with a price and the blood of JESUS is the price.
He paid the greatest price in all creation for this "HIM in us/us in HIM" fused relationship.
In this blood-bought state, we live and we move and we have our being IN HIM.
We are IN HIM, created with free will to choose, the "yes" or the "no", free to decide.
GOD is at work within us, giving us both the desire, the joy, and the ability to participate with HIM in this IN HIM life (Phil. 2:13).

Everything in GOD flows from the revelation that HE created us to be one IN HIM (John 17:20-28).
This IN HIM life is the continual process of "LORD, flood the eyes of our hearts with light so we know and understand the hope, the reality of this calling, and the surpassing greatness of your power in and for us who believe" (Eph. 1:17-23).

1.2 Who are you?

The answer to the question, "Who are you, who are you, and do you know who you are?" is . . .

You are the righteousness of GOD in CHRIST JESUS, so just as HE is right now, you are in the world.

You are HIS feet, you are HIS body, you are HIS limbs, and you are HIS voice, right now.

There is no separation. There is no distance.

There is nothing that divides, separates, or distances you from HIM, so the truth is that as HE is right now, you are in the world.

So, you are just like HIM.

The difference is, He's the I AM, with a glorified body, and you have a mortal body, which is quickened now by that same SPIRIT that raised CHRIST from the dead.

You are Lazarus, whether you know it or not.

Lazarus was raised to die a physical death again, but you are raised to eternal life, never to die again.

You have already died with CHRIST in GOD.

You are already risen to resurrection life with CHRIST in GOD, and you are already risen and seated with CHRIST in GOD.

The evidence of our senses tells us this is impossible, but the wonder of it is that it's real and true.

In HIM it is already accomplished, written, done, and the discussion is over.

So, you live and move and have your being, your existence, in the realm of "of course it's impossible, but never with HIM", ever.

So, this life here is "get over it, it's already covered".

1.3 Our blood covenant relationship

This is about the New Covenant.
This is the lifting up of down here.
The New Covenant lifts us up to the higher ground, to the reality of what HE did with HIS body and blood.
This blood covenant lifts us up so we're not stuck down here.
This New Covenant was declared for us, given to us, and validated for us by the blood of JESUS.
A blood covenant means that the two parties involved in this agreement become inseparable and the covenant is unbreakable.
The blood shared in order to validate the covenant was the blood of JESUS, which was both the blood of man and the blood of GOD.

So, the agreement is between man and GOD.
This covenant establishes and declares our relationship.
It's a covenant of relationship between man and GOD, **it is simply HIM in us and us in HIM.**
It's a union of two realms being fused together, natural and supernatural.
GOD in man, and man in GOD. The impossible merging of two realms that cannot be joined.
The impossible made possible.

The direct result of this fusion is that all that one party has, belongs also to the other party.
So, what we have of this earth that now belongs to JESUS, is our freedom to walk on this earth, as HE leads.
We take HIM to where HE wants to go on this earth, for wherever we are so HE is.
HE does the work that HE does, because our feet take HIM to where HE wants to do that work.
And HE uses our mouth, or our hands, or whatever part of us is required, because that is our relationship.
That is what we have given to HIM in this covenant relationship.

What HE has given to us is the freedom from whatever device Satan could possibly put on us.

HE gave us freedom from all these devices in this relationship, so we live, and move, and have our being in HIM, now.

HE gives us understanding of this supernatural realm which is so foreign to our natural understanding.

This place where HE seated us is where we are like HIM, and is bought with New Covenant blood.

We have HIS authority to declare what HE'S already accomplished, as done on the earth.

The flesh puts up the argument that these satanic attacks are here and are to be feared.

"How dare you say it's finished, and everything you need is right there. How dare you say that?"

They are perceived by the senses, in the sense realm, to still be there, even though HE says they have been taken.

But this is the sense realm.

This is the realm of change, where anything and everything is subject to change.

Whereas the supernatural realm, the Spirit realm, is a realm where all is fixed and unchangeable, and is filled with truth.

So, when the truth is spoken, changes occur in the natural realm.

Changes are made in the natural realm by the WORD going into the Spirit realm, the WORD of GOD.

So, we use what HE has given us, without fear.

1.4 The basics of life IN HIM

"HE whom the SON sets free is free indeed."
But in this day in the Body of CHRIST, this has been dumbed down to feeling good, to emotional good, or happy thoughts.
It's been so dumbed down that there is fear and struggle every time there is an attack of any kind.
In this walk, anything that attacks your life, the life of JESUS in you repels.

The elements of the communion, the body and the blood, are powerful.
JESUS said, "Take, eat, this is MY body broken for you," and "Drink this, this is MY blood of the new covenant to set men free."
The revelation of the power of the communion, the looking at it, the eating of it, and the drinking of it, denies the right of the devil to say or do anything in your life. He has no rights over you!
The devil is a defeated foe.
We say that in the Body of CHRIST with little recognition of what it really means.
It means we have the potential of walking in freedom from bondage, and freedom from any kind of fear.
It's nothing less than the full complement of what JESUS has done in sacrificing HIS life for us.

This truth is the essence of a life of freedom from any attack of the devil: sickness, fear, condemnation, lack.
All this was made absolute in the finished work of JESUS on the cross.
The body and the blood repel any thought that you deserve bad things.
We are seated with HIM, having died with HIM, risen with HIM, and now seated with HIM.
It's as if the HOLY SPIRIT has to lift you up to see who you already are.
This body and blood are so profound in who HE'S made us to be. The Body of CHRIST.
It's so profound that as HE is, so are we.
We are filled with power.
Filled with dunamis.

Filled with resurrection power.

We are filled with supernatural power, to say and to speak what HE has already accomplished.

It's not a mind game, it's not anything else but the full work of the cross and the resurrection.

Therefore, the devil can have no say in the running of our life on this earth.

We get to say, "NO! Shut up! It's already done. I don't give you the time of day. The discussion is actually OVER, I'm not listening, go away, I'm free."

The devil is seeking whom he may devour, constantly, all the time.

He never shuts up because he can't, because he's a spirit.

But we have the HOLY SPIRIT inside these vessels to rule and reign over him because of the body and blood of JESUS.

It's not because of what we think about ourselves, or of anybody else's experience.

The strength and power of JESUS' body and blood gives us the right to resist, and that's why you can resist.

The power of this body and blood is earth shattering.

It's earth shaking.

It's bondage breaking.

It absolutely sets us free from anything that would beset us while we're here.

That's why the viper is shaken off, back into the flame from whence it came.

Shaken off.

Anything that would beset us shaken off, back where it came from.

JESUS gave us the right to do that.

1.5 Your place IN HIM

You can't see it, you can't measure it, you can't control it or manage it.

The blood of JESUS is at work in your physical body every single second that you are here.

This resurrection life is in you because the life is in the blood and you are in HIM and HIS blood is in you.

HIS blood in you is working this work, this resurrection life work, this cleansing, renewing, restoring, and redeeming work.

This washing of the water by the WORD work, washing and washing, is a continuous process.

It continues when you're asleep, and when you're awake.

It continues when you're aware of it, and when you're not aware of it.

It continues when you're worshipping, and when you're simply walking through your day.

It's all the time, and it never stops.

It's HIS idea and HE thought you up before the foundation of the world.

He thought up this whole eternal, resurrection life.

HIS blood and HIS body are a demonstration of what HE has done to all the principalities and powers and rulers of wickedness in high places.

At the same time, the two realms, the physical and the spiritual, are in concert not in opposition, because HE made it that way.

HE designed it that way, so HIS life could be in our mortal bodies, working, restoring, redeeming, renewing, quickening.

It is done with the WORD, washing, and washing, and washing, and washing.

Every need is washed in this reality of HIS life inside your body while you're here.

And it's while you're here that this body needs HIS quickening because in your glorified body it's a done deal!

This is the quickening time down here, where you're quickened by that same SPIRIT that raised CHRIST from the dead.

Died with HIM, risen with HIM, seated with HIM.

You are the righteousness of GOD in CHRIST.

You are like HIM while you're here, with HIS life inside your physical being.
HE is working, and washing, and renewing, and restoring, and redeeming.
Constantly kept **IN HIM.**
Constantly kept by HIS life.

HE reveals HIMSELF to you in whatever way you personally need the revelation of the body and the blood.
HE delights in you knowing and being in HIM because it's HIS plan and purpose, and His plan and purpose is eternal.
It is eternal in origin, in nature, and in demonstration.
It will be fulfilled because HIS word is already settled on whatever the issue happens to be.

1.6 I put myself into you

Who do you think I am?
Who do YOU think I am?
Who do you think I AM?
I'm not like you.
I am not moved by anything at all.

Who do you think I am?
Look at who I AM.
I do not behave like you.
I put myself into you, you didn't put yourself into me.
I took everything that would in any way limit or damage you.
I AM, I AM, I AM.
I did not withhold or spare even my own SON but gave HIM up for you all, how will I not with HIM, freely, graciously give you all other things.

Who do you think I am?
I AM not a man that would lie, or change my mind about you, about what I've done.
Look at who I AM, what I AM like, not what you are like.
Not an earthly father, nothing to do with the earth.
You're looking at lack all the time, being moved by lack in any form, but I did not even spare my own SON but gave HIM up for you, and will not withhold any good thing from you.
That's who I AM!

You withhold all the time in order to control, but I'm already "I AM".
That's why every time a person looks at me for a second, they're changed!
Looking at who I AM, they're changed from death to life, they're changed!
Eternally they're changed and their lives are turned upside down, inside out.
Their lives are changed in that moment, in that looking at who I AM, they see themselves in relationship to me, and they're changed in that second of looking.

That's why this life, the fight of faith, is not what is taught.
The fight of faith is the looking,
The looking at who I AM.
The moment of the looking changes everything and enables the supernatural to transform the natural.

You're completely transformed in the looking, in the looking and the seeing.
As soon as you see for a second, you're changed.
Every time, your inside vision is seeing something else, you're stuck and limited to down here and you can't get free of it.
The moment you look at who I AM everything is possible.
Every single thing is possible.
There is nothing that is impossible in the looking, the seeing.
That's why the looking at what's seen all the time, the focusing on it, the looking at it, the measuring it, and the counting it is so draining.
It drains the life out of you.
The hope is gone, and the joy is gone, and the peace is gone, because there's nothing of those things in the looking.
There's only more and more and more looking.
Again and again and again and again.
There's only more looking at the what's down here, and how it looks, and how it should be, and all those other things.
As soon as you look at who I AM, nothing is withheld.
Nothing is withheld from you while you're on the earth.
Nothing!

1.7 The reality of the IN HIM life

This life "IN HIM", where we live and we move and we have our being "IN HIM", is not the place that we think it is.
It's not the place that we have been told that it is.
This life "IN HIM" has nothing to do with all the structure and the containment of men.
This place "IN HIM" will not conform to man's ideas of what it is.
It is impossible for it to conform to a natural structure because this place in HIM is HIS supernatural life.
It does not and will not be normal. It will not behave. It will not.
It cannot because HIS life is filled with HIM, filled with HIS love, and filled with HIS light.
For GOD is light and GOD is love.
JESUS did not conform, so this life "IN HIM" will not conform and is not containable. It will not be contained.
HE did not conform.
HE took all the pressure of the conforming and all the demand of "you must".
All the demand, HE took it all in HIMSELF.

HE became the curse for us, so we're not under the curse. It has no place in this "IN HIM" life.
So therefore, any of the judging, shaming, cursing, damning, constraining, constricting, and limiting, will simply burst its bonds.
It will burst out because resurrection life bursts out, and so the believer's life will not look like anyone else's life.
It cannot, because HE paid the price with HIS blood for this life that will not fit. It won't fit.
It won't be fitted into a mould to be replicated.
That's why this life is so filled with HIS power and filled with HIS demonstration of signs and miracles and wonders.
This life, HIS life in us, cannot be contained. It's like a cork that cannot be put back into the bottle because it bursts out with life.
There's no other way for this "IN HIM" life to express itself.

This "IN HIM" life where we live and move and have our being is entirely opposite to what we see.

It's the opposite of the thing we see in front of us.

The blood of Jesus has already spoken on all of it.

JESUS said, "It is finished," so all the demands to live this life in the normal, in the flesh, and in the natural, is finished.

HE finished that, so that's over.

So, we thank you for it LORD, we thank you for it.

YOU flood the eyes of our hearts with light in the whole Body of CHRIST, so we start to see who YOU are and who we are.

In YOU we live, we move, and we have our being. It's entirely different . . .

1.8 MY strength, not yours

Man always thinks that his strength has to be his strength, but I say my strength is your strength.
Your weakness is the opportunity for MY strength to pour in and be manifested.
So every time you experience weakness, MY strength pours in and changes that weakness into strength.
It's supernatural strength.
It's strength to do whatever the day requires.
It's different from you, man, being strong.

MY strength is made perfect in weakness, it is perfected in weakness.
It is perfect because I designed you to make you to be completely reliant on me.
I give you the physical strength.
I give you emotional strength.
I give you spiritual strength.
I give you every kind of strength, to live this life, to live every single day that you are here.
It is not in your own strength.
It is never in your own strength.
It is the same SPIRIT that raised CHRIST from the dead that quickens your mortal body while you are here.
Quickening and enabling you to do that which you cannot do.

In fact, you are strong in the LORD and in the power of HIS might.
YOU are strong in the LORD and the power of HIS might.
You can do all things through CHRIST who strengthens you.
You are more than a conqueror through HIM that loves you because as HE is, so are you in the world.
You are filled with resurrection life in this body right now.
Every day that you're here, you are filled with the life of GOD.
That same spirit that raised CHRIST from the dead quickens your mortal, earthbound, earth-born body.

It quickens your earth-born body right now, so that as HE is, so are you in this world right now.

You are filled with GOD.

You are filled with HIS resurrection life.

You are filled with HIS ability.

You are filled with HIS wisdom.

You are filled with HIS righteousness.

You are set apart, sanctified in HIM.

You are redeemed because of HIM.

HE is made unto you all things that are necessary for this life and godliness.

Every single thing.

1.9 Treasures in earthen vessels

The reason why we are treasures in earthen vessels is so that the excellence and the demonstration of the power would be of GOD. The reason would be of GOD and not of ourselves.

These divine things are given to you to say in this earthen vessel of clay, in this body, on the earth.

The divine things that you get to say give HIM praise, attention, and adoration.

Your words, declarations, and proclamations, give HIM praise, attention, and adoration.

We are demonstrations of the wonder of HIS creation and HIS life.

The six water pots at the wedding in Cana were made of clay that HE created.

The container is HIS creation.

The water is HIS creation, and the water is changed by HIS supernatural intervention.

To whomever you speak, wherever you go, HIS life in you is the supply.

HIS supply of joy.

HIS supply of peace.

The speaking and the being of HIM in the earth.

You are in that sense, HIS supply to someone else.

You are a container of HIM, but your body is part of the supply in the whole body of CHRIST, one to another.

One to another.

One to another, all over the face of the earth.

So that's why you can freely go, and freely receive, and freely give because of CHRIST in you.

CHRIST in you, the hope, and the reality of glory, is HIS life on earth in these vessels.

In these containers of HIM.

1.10 Living by the promptings

The disciples came to JESUS and said, "What about him, what about the other guys?"
JESUS said, "Well, what is that to you, you follow ME."

Now, YOU follow MY promptings because I am in you and I shed MY blood to be in you.
It's the most expensive commodity in all of creation and I paid the price for this reality.
Therefore, you don't have to look at someone else to teach you who I made you to be.
Because the blood I shed for you is in you, and the anointing is within you.
The Holy Ghost inside you teaches you.
It's true, you have no need to have any man teach you how to be who I made you to be.

Nobody wants to hear this but it's not about obeying.
HE took all the demand for obeying.
It's just about being.
It's just about being IN HIM.

I took all the demand in MY body and I was broken by it and I shed MY blood for it.
I did the whole thing so all the demand of obedience is already paid for.
So, I just prompt you.
You don't try to be yourself today, you just are yourself.

Body of CHRIST, you've been sold a bill of goods, wow!
Sold a bill of goods.
Before the cross they had to obey, because if they didn't they got whapped!
There were bad consequences then, but I took all those consequences.
The whole Body of CHRIST is running around obeying, but I say, "Come on, let's go over here, let's BE over here."

The thing is you can choose either fork in the road, and we go there together.
I am in you and I took all the fear and the consequences of getting it wrong.

There can be no fear in MY love because there IS no fear in MY love.
Even if you do the same thing you did before – there's no fear in my love.
I took it on your behalf, so you're free to be who I made you to be.
Just rest in that.
Simple!

CHAPTER 2
Living This Impossible Life

2.1 Without ME you can't do it

How can I prove to you who I am if you can do it?

That's why you live in a state that seems impossible, for without ME you cannot do it.

That's why I made you a new creature in ME, so you can live this way that's impossible.

That's why I made you a new creature, so I can continually prove to you who I am.

For without ME you can do nothing, and with ME you can do all things.

You can't make yourself a new creature, it's not given to you. Step out of your humanity IN ME.

There is no other way to live while you are here on earth. No other way, no other place, because it is finished.

Remember I said, "Come, follow me and I will make you fishers of men."

You don't make yourself.

Just leave all the "making yourself" to ME.

You live and move and have your being in ME.

In ME is the real place of rest from all the trying, because it is only ME who can make you.

2.2 Doing the impossible

There is a reason in GOD for the impossibility of it all.

The impossibility of stepping out on water, where the placing of the foot on the water, on the impossible, causes the impossible to become possible. It is at that moment of impact, of the stepping onto the water, when it cannot reasonably, rationally, or logically sustain and support the weight of the decision to step out, that the impossible becomes possible.

The decision is made to do the impossible, expecting the impossible to be manifested in the realm where it is not in evidence, and it is every single time, at the eleventh hour seemingly, that the impossible becomes possible.

There is reason in GOD, that HE shows HIMSELF strong on your behalf where you are unable to do anything other than make the decision to lift your foot and place it on the water which will not sustain or support you. It's in that acting out of the thing that's in the heart.

It always has been, stepping out and doing the impossible by simply stepping on the water, which will not sustain or support because it cannot.

In every circumstance and every situation, there is this stepping out on the water when HE says, "Come."

So, you come and you step out on that which is unsustainable, and unsupportable, and just has nothing there.

It is that stepping out, which is that calling into being those things which are not as though they were.

That's what this is.

It's the mouth of the fish.

It's Peter's miraculous deliverance from prison.

It's water turned into wine.

It is every single time where the impossible is in evidence.

It is in the moment of decision to act on the WORD that is in the heart, where everything changes. And that is it.

Just as JESUS only did what HE saw the FATHER do, so are you in the world.

Water is for walking on!

2.3 It cannot be reasonable

This being led by the SPIRIT will not conform.
This life of being led by the SPIRIT will not be reasonable.
It will not conform. It is unreasonable every single time.
You are unable to be reasonable, because HE lives in you.
That's why the "widow and the mite".
That's why the "speaking to the waves".
That's why the "money in the mouth of the fish".
That's why the "prison doors open of their own accord".
That's why, that's why, that's why.
So, every single time you try to be reasonable, it won't work, because there's no life in it.
The cross – unreasonable!
The resurrection – unreasonable!

Up from the grave HE arose, a mighty triumph o'er HIS foes, HE arose the victor from the dark domain and HE lives forever with HIS saints to reign, HE arose, HE arose, CHRIST JESUS arose.

This resurrection life will not conform. It will not conform. It just won't.
Every time you try to alter your behavior by being reasonable, it won't work.
That's why JESUS only did what HE saw the FATHER doing, in heaven, outside the realm of the reasonable.
So, get over it! This trying to be reasonable about your behaviour down here.
Reasonable says one way, but it's always at odds with this life in the SPIRIT because it can't be any other way.

2.4 This life is not what it looks like

It's all about this life.

It all comes down to it, and it has nothing to do with what it looks like, or anyone's perception of what it looks like.

It's nothing to do with what it looks like.

The outward has nothing to do with what the reality is.

It has nothing to do with it. It's just outward casing.

It's just like a covering, that's all it is.

He chooses the covering, the uniform, and the equipment that HE wants. He puts the desire in you for that uniform, covering, and outward appearance because of the people that it gives you entrance with.

That's all it is.

All the uniform of this life, all the dressing for the occasion, all the superficial appearance is just dressing.

That's all it is.

2.5 I do it MY way

This impossible life which I designed for MY Body on the earth, is impossible to live in any other way without complete reliance on the HEAD to be the HEAD, to be the brains of the outfit, to be the ONE who leads, and guides, and empowers, and heals, and delivers, and saves, and provides in every single way.

Because I'M the head of MY Church, I do the work within MY Church, and within MY Body.
It does not conform to the way one would think it should be from looking at it down here.
I do it MY way.
It is MY way, and it's filled with light, and it's filled with love.
There's never any condemnation.
There's never any fear.
There's never any distancing.
There's never any of that because it's MY Body.

This expression of what I do, demonstrates ME in MY Body and how I do it.
So, all the activity, and exertion, and exhaustion of you trying to do it comes to naught.
It comes to nothing because I do all the work and it's completely different.
The body's part is just to be the body, and not the Head who decides how it should be, how it looks, how it functions, or how it reacts.
It's simply MY life, in MY Body, demonstrating ME.
I will use whatever I want in this world as bait to capture men's hearts that I made for ME to dwell in while physical bodies are on the earth.
I will use whatever, anything and everything.

2.6 Having your being IN HIM

This life IN HIM is actually simple.
This life IN HIM is not complicated.
It's not difficult. It's not hard. It's not a burden.
This life IN HIM is not a struggle.
It's actually simple.
This life IN HIM is the opposite of what it seems to be to the flesh.
The flesh cannot apprehend it, grasp it, understand it, or bring it into order.
So, it is difficult and unwieldy and unreasonable and illogical and foolish to the flesh.
The things of GOD are foolish to the flesh by nature.
So, the grappling with it in the flesh to bring it into some kind of demonstrable order is very frustrating.
It will not be grappled with because it's simple.
IN HIM you live, you move, and you have your being.

It's simple, so when HE says, "Go and look in the mouth of a fish," you go and look in the mouth of a fish.
It's simple because there is the provision.
HE says, "Go . . ." and there's the provision, and it's simple.

It does not behave in an orderly, natural fashion because it's not natural, it's supernatural.
The simplicity of it is in the supernatural.
IN HIM you live and move and have your being.
It demonstrates HIM.
IN HIM is found the simplicity of it.
IN HIM is found the joy.
IN HIM is the release of it.
It truly is the exact opposite of what it looks like down here.
That's why you look and focus on the things that are unseen, not the things that are seen.
You reckon yourself dead to those things of the world.

You reckon yourself dead to how it operates and how it looks down here. They do not regulate how you live IN HIM, and move IN HIM, and have your being IN HIM.

It's just a very simple life when HE says, "I've already done it."

So you say, "Thank you, it's mine, it's already done."

And you go on with your day.

IN HIM it's always the suspension of the natural.

The natural is suspended in the overriding, overruling, and overwhelming flow of the supernatural.

It's suspended.

It's stopped in its tracks.

It has no other way or ability to stop or hinder or pervert.

All those things that the natural constantly says it can do are absolutely swept away as the supernatural suspends the natural.

It's suspended in this life IN HIM, where you live and move and have your being.

So, you call these things that are not as if they are, and that suspends the natural.

HIS action of putting HIMSELF in us suspends the natural.

It's putting the supernatural into the natural vessel.

We take in the supernatural, so the natural no longer controls the "IN HIM" life.

It's seeing that, and living that, and having your being in that reality where the things seen do not control us.

Instead it's always the unseen.

It's always what you cannot see in the natural.

That's what this life is about.

2.7 These are the days

These are the days. These are the times.

In former days GOD spoke through prophets, but in these days HE speaks through HIS SON.

HIS speaking reveals.

HIS speaking unblocks the ears.

HIS speaking opens eyes to see.

It's HIS speaking through the SON. Through the "it is finished", through the blood.

The blood speaks of it, the blood declares it, the blood gives account of the finished work of JESUS.

The work is completed, so these are the days of the SON speaking through the cross and through the resurrection.

The SON speaks through HIS life blood.

The resurrection life in the blood flows continually, never stopping.

These days are the days that speak.

These days have a voice that opens ears and opens eyes. They open to see differently.

They start to see what this life is in both realms simultaneously.

This existing in two realms at once. No division. No separating of it, in these days.

In these days, it is holding fast to HIM. Holding fast to the Head of the Body.

There is no other place from which to derive or draw this life.

There's no other place and there's no other being. For it is HIS Body.

HIS life will never conform to the earthly because it cannot.

It's of a different origin, a different nature, a different species, and a different being.

This is a simultaneous existence, this being "in HIM", this living and moving and having our being in HIM.

Trying to make this life work is like trying to put the square peg into a round hole, and it will never work because it cannot work.

It's a different nature and so it will not work.

Because of that, the stepping out into these days needed a gifting to do it, and HE gave HIMSELF for that purpose.

To step out from the force of it.

To step out from the pressure of it.

To step out from the tyranny of it.

To step into the fulfillment of it.

It took THE gift of GOD Himself for you to step into the IN HIM life of "you have not chosen ME but I have chosen you to go forth and to bear fruit, and your fruit will remain so that whatever you ask the FATHER in MY NAME, HE will do it," and "if one lives or one dies, what is that to you, you follow me."

It's a gifting and a calling because there is no ability to do this in the natural.

I did it for you, just go on with your day.

2.8 HE's doing a new thing

This new thing, it's a new thing, you haven't done this before so there's no precedent, there's no formula, there's no checking all the boxes, and there's no path that's already trodden for you to follow.

So, it's breaking out into new territory for you, and you can't figure it out because it will not be figured out.

You think you see and understand some things, but it's a new thing that HE does, and it's HIS life.

It blows you. It's like the wind on a sailboat. It blows you into places where you haven't been before.

You thought it was one place and HE has another place.

You look at one place and that seems like the perfect solution, but HE blows this sailboat.

HE fills the sails with HIS wind, and blows you somewhere else and you land somewhere you didn't expect to land.

But it's HIS wind, and it's HIS wind, and it's new and it springs forth.

This is a new thing in the SPIRIT, and in this dispensation of the SPIRIT, and of the blood where it's all finished.

So, it looks entirely different, because HE is doing a new thing.

You can't plan shelving in this move of the SPIRIT, and you can't plan where everything's going to go on the shelves.

This is different. That was then and this is now, and you can't plan that.

So, you can't plan that in the way you would plan it.

In HIS plan and HIS purpose you simply put one foot in front of the other and you walk into HIS plan.

Then all the shelving will be in the right place, and everything will absolutely be put on the right shelf at the right time.

It will be done in HIS way and everything will be perfect about it, so there's no fussing about it.

It really is Ephesians 2:10: "You are His workmanship, created in Christ Jesus, born from above that you would walk in the paths that HE has preordained for you to walk in" (paraphrase by authors).

Off you go. Just walk, enjoy your day.

2.9 This is who I AM and this is what life in the SPIRIT is

This is the place.

This is the place that HE has prepared for you, where you simply put one foot in front of the other.

This is the place where you participate by giving your body to it. For HE has made your physical body as a wrapping.

He inside you and you in HIM. For in HIM you live and move and have your being.

It's the giving of your body to it and the releasing of your body to it.

It's the members of your body, and of your voice, and of your physical self, saying "yes, yes, this is who I am."

This is what this life is. It's the living and moving and having my being in HIM.

Your participation is this vessel, like those water pots, like the six water pots.

The vessel where the water was poured into, so that the transformation could be facilitated.

So that HE could demonstrate who HE is in that vessel, by the pouring out of the wine from that vessel.

This is a life of "HE pours it in and it pours out".

And there's no cessation of it and there's no diminishing of it because it's a simple life process.

The blood has already done the work for this kind of "pouring out life".

Where your mind doesn't shut it down and say that this is stupid and ridiculous and opens me to ridicule.

HIS life inside simply pours out, it pours in and pours out anyway, because there is life in the blood.

Because the blood has already redeemed and set aside these vessels where HIS life is inside.

It is a drink for all and when they drink, they'll never thirst again.

They'll never thirst again, because these waters are supplied by the blood of the Lamb, and so it's different.

That's why the participation of your body, your physical being, your voice, your breath, is the reality of your life in HIM.

That's why your assent to it is the "yes and amen" in CHRIST JESUS.

All the promises, all the place, all the reality is in the participation of it, your own flesh, your own breath.

So, every single experience of this life is like a demonstration.

Your body and your physical being are like a demonstration of HIS life inside the physical covering, the wrapping.

The world says this is ridiculous and it opens you to ridicule.

But it must be open to ridicule, because there's no other way for this life, except to be open to ridicule.

HIS blood stops any condemnation and stops the shame of the exposure to ridicule, and simply barrels on through anyway.

This life is where your choice moves from the "no" to the "yes", where everything flows from, over, and over, and over again.

It always flows because this is how it works in the SPIRIT.

The disciples came and said, "LORD, how are we supposed to do what GOD wants us to do? How are we supposed to work this thing? How are we supposed to do this?" And JESUS said, "Believe on the One that HE sent."

Over, and over again. It's the same thing, because this is how the SPIRIT works. This is how this life in the SPIRIT works. The mouth of the fish is ridiculous. This is how it works.

HE's always going to say, "Go and look in the mouth of the fish." That's how it is. That's how it always is.

Go and fill the empty water pots with water and at some point, between the movement of the servants taking the water to fill the water pots, and the scooping out of the "give the people a drink from it", it's changed.

So, this is how it works. It's the same deal. JESUS, the WORD of GOD, was with GOD always.

In the beginning was the WORD, and the WORD was with GOD and the WORD was GOD, and the WORD became flesh.

The WORD dwelt among us and we beheld HIS glory of the only begotten SON of the FATHER, who is full of grace and truth, who came and was clothed with a physical form.

Same deal, always. The WORD comes and it's wrapped in physical form. So, go and do the irrational, the ridiculous, that which makes no sense.

It's the improbable and impossible, all the time. Every single time. That's how it works.

It's at HIS WORD, and HIS WORD comes in a thought. It just comes in a thought. That's all it is.

CHAPTER 3
Being Led

3.1 I am the good Shepherd

I am the good SHEPHERD.
I am the one that leads you into pastures that are green.
They are pastures where you feed and where you're nourished.
I lead you to where there are still waters where your soul is restored.
Because I am the good SHEPHERD.
I know how to lead you there.

You don't know how to lead, but I know how to lead.
I know how to lead and I am leading you into pastures that are food for you.
I'm giving you nourishment, and quickening.
I give you everything that you need right now, while you're here.
Everything that you need is in these pasture lands that I've prepared for you.
I lead you into that place of nourishment, and health, and quickening, and everything that you need.
I quicken you to where there are still waters for you to drink of and be restored.
That's what I do!

Because I love you!

3.2 I will show you and you will go

For you have not walked this way before.
You haven't walked on this path before.
You haven't walked this way before, so there's nothing that you can compare it to or judge it by.
There is nothing in the past that has any reference to what it is now.
Not yesterday, not ten years ago, not twenty, thirty, forty, or fifty years ago.
Nothing.

Nothing at all, because they are paths which I will show and you will go.
I will show and you will go.
So, it's not in your head because it's being led.
So, I will do it and you will know it.
When I show it to your heart, that's your part.
I will show and you will go.
So, stop it. Don't even look at it because I will show and you will go.
And that's all you need to know.

So, the days are coming when you will see
What I have put in place for thee.
The days are coming when you will know
Where I will send you and you will go.
There is no fear because this time has come near.
So never draw back because of perceived lack.
For I will supply wherever and however I call you to release what I've put inside.
Because it is MY supply.

It really is John 15:16 about your life.

3.3 Doors

HE has doors for you to walk through, so you walk up to the door and the door opens of its own accord.

The door simply opens and there's no forcing and there's nothing required by you in order to open the door.

All you do is walk up to it.

Your part is getting your body up to the doors, and they open of their own accord.

It's not an angel that opens the door and it's not a human being.

HE opens the door which has in fact been closed until this day.

Today the door opens to you and you walk through into HIS abundant provision that is already bought and paid for.

It's already bought and paid for.

Because HIS body was broken, your body is whole.

Anything that would break you has now been dealt with.

You just walk through the door that is open because of HIS body and HIS blood.

The door simply opens before you into HIS provision.

HIS provision is abundance, extravagance, and ostentatious supply.

Just because of what HE wants to do in you and for you and with you.

What HE wants to do is ostentatious, which is a word that the flesh recoils from, but the heart runs to.

This is a heart that knows the GOD who spoke the worlds into being, and that's ostentatious.

It's a heart that knows the GOD who sent HIS own son.

Who sent HIM to become flesh and dwell among us, full of grace and truth.

This is GOD's ostentatious response to man's dilemma.

This is GOD's ostentatious show to principalities and powers and rulers of wickedness in high places.

See what I have done.

See who I AM.

Ostentatious.

3.4 Walking through the door

When the door is open, there are no barriers.
There's an open door for, there's an open door for the gift of GOD.
Moving out and moving out in it and into it.
In HIM, it's a moving out because the door is open.
You simply move out, it's an open door.

There are many adversaries, but the adversaries all say the same thing:
"Did HE really say . . .?"
The adversaries always say the same thing.
They stir up fear saying, "Is HE going to? Is HE really going to do what
HE said HE's going to do?"
The adversaries always say the same thing.

The door is open for you to go and to move because HE is in you.
Because HE's in you, when you move, HE is in the move.
Whenever you move, wherever you move to or take your feet to, go
through the door because GOD is in you.
GOD walks through that door, so it simply is walking through the open
door with HIM and then all these things are added.
They're all added because they're all done.
It's all because HE's in you and you're in HIM.
You just walk through it and you move out through the door into HIS
plan and purpose.

So, it's easy. It's as easy as one foot in front of the other, and that's what it
is.
This is walking through into HIS provision, and the adversaries say it's
into nothing, but HE says it's into HIS provision.
You walk into HIS abundant provision and into the place where everything
is taken care.
A place where everything is orchestrated for you.

You're walking through the door and the adversaries say, "Oh there's nothing on the other side. You're walking into nothing."

That's a lie, and GOD is not man that HE should lie.

Because HE's in you and you are in HIM, it's always there.

You're walking into HIS complete provision.

He sends people to come to aid and to help, people that HE's called.

People that HE's called to be part of this walking through the door and into HIS provision.

Walking out of the constriction and walking through the door and into the larger, into the bigger, into the expanse of it.

Just walking, stepping over the threshold and there it all is.

3.5 You have not chosen me but . . .

These days are unlike any other days.
They are because you've not chosen ME, but I have chosen you to go forth
and bear fruit and that your fruit remains.
It's not up to you to produce the fruit.
It's not up to you to make the fruit remain.
You didn't do the choosing. You didn't do the equipping. You didn't do the
calling. You didn't do the production of fruit.
All your part is "in HIM you live and you move and you have your being".
That's your part.

These days are unlike any other.
These are days of looking at the next step and wondering how can it be
that this is what is in your heart.
These are days of the going forth and being thrust out with such a
propelling inside.
This propulsion to do it is because of the time it is.
Before it was working on one side of the boat all the time.
Now it's the other side of the boat.
The propulsion to do it is "you go forth and you will bear fruit and your
fruit will remain, so that whatever you ask the FATHER in MY Name HE
will do it," and it is as simple as that.

It's not complex, it's not complicated, and it's not difficult, but it is the
other side of the boat.
It is all the things that you know in your heart are absolutely true and
right.
So, it is the propulsion to go to that because it's the SPIRIT of GOD
propelling, and because these days are specific days.

These are specific days, and they are just for this little period of time, and
there will be a propulsion out.

The things that are in readiness here now may completely change, because these are the days that you're in.

HE thought it, and these days are chosen and appointed because of HIS purpose.

3.6 You thought you did it

You have the mind of CHRIST in this IN HIM life.
So, as a man thinketh in his heart, so he is.
Because I am in your heart, so I think, and you think.

So, you thought you made big decisions in your life because they were good ideas, and because you thought them.
But I say I thought them.
You say you thought it, but I say I thought it.
It was MY idea.
So, this day that you're in, I thought it.

MY thoughts are in your thoughts.
That's why whatever you say, you have, because MY thoughts are in your thoughts, and that is the reality.
That is the reality and there is no other reality.

So, you can give yourself with full joy and abandon to your thinking, because your gifts and callings are MY thoughts.
They're not your thoughts.
So, they don't look like anybody else's thoughts.

CHAPTER 4
The Time is Now

4.1 The time is now

For surely the time is now. The day is now.

You will see MY hand extended in a measure you have never seen before.

For I am making a way where there is no other way.

Let that truth and that word fill and flood your understanding.

The way will open before you and you will see the provision on every hand.

Anointing, prosperity, joy, peace, and answers on every hand.

Opening up your heart's desire.

I AM in every corner of your life, so rejoice for I AM the WAY.

I AM the TRUTH.

I AM the LIFE.

I AM the ANSWER.

I AM the FAITHFUL ONE.

I AM the ETERNAL ONE.

I AM the COUNSELLOR.

I AM the ONE who never fails.

I AM the ONE who loves you perfectly, and I AM the ONE who casts out all fear.

I AM.

4.2 We walk in the expectation

Trust ME and do not be afraid of change because I am doing a new thing.
Therefore, do not be afraid.
The change is the demonstration of the call.
Everything necessary for the call is provided.
Because of the call, HE has prepared the fulfillment of the time, and increase, and overflow.

In previous revivals, HE prepared the people.
It was the work of the HOLY GHOST where people were called and went to a certain place to receive what their hearts desired.

This thing is in some way part of the leading up to the end.
This thing is part of the process of the coming again of the LORD JESUS.
Just as the rapture is a part of the process, it is all a part of the process.
So, walk in the expectation with eyes open and ears open for the sights and the sounds.
For you will hear and you will see the changes being brought about, and you will be part of the changes being brought about.
HE is revealing just a little bit, a little bit to get us ready for the next day, only one day at a time.
It's because of the call.
It's because of the plan.
It's because of the purpose.

4.3 Seeing things differently

In this time.

It's an hour, and a day, and a time of looking and seeing differently.

Of looking, and seeing, and perceiving, and understanding differently.

This hour that you're in is a leaving behind of the things that are behind.

At this hour, that you're in, it's a looking and seeing and perceiving differently.

You cannot see, or perceive, or understand the way you did before, because this hour is the hour you're brought to.

It is, in fact, a different hour.

It's a different thing because of the life that's in you.

Restored. Renewed. Replenished. Redeemed.

Everything in this life looks different, so you speak those things which are not as though they are.

The redemption, and the fulfillment, and the restoration, and the replenishing are received as done.

So, you can't look, or perceive, or judge the way you did before.

It's about expectation.

Expecting. Absolutely expecting the word of "it's finished, I've got you covered" to be demonstrated.

The demonstration of it, the walking into it, the reception of it, and of the immersion into it.

The demonstration of "I have it covered", just walk into it and receive it without a thought of not receiving it.

Without a thought of it not being manifested, of it not being reality in the material realm, in the physical realm.

Fear keeps you out of walking into the fullness of the natural provision, of the "I've got it done."

I am GOD of the natural and the supernatural.

I am GOD of all of it, so you just walk into the reality of that.

I smooth the way for you, so it's not a struggle.
It's not a struggle.
I took the struggle, so you just walk in freedom.
I took the struggle.
I just took the struggle, so it's not your struggle.

4.4 The ice blocks are cracking

This work that HE's doing of waking up the body from this somnambulant state, this sleeping state, is akin to the Herodian foundation stones, but with blocks that are made out of ice.

When the HOLY GHOST and fire are applied, or are in the area, the fire starts, and fissures and cracks start to resound within these Herodian-sized ice blocks.

Everything that is not built on JESUS CHRIST will melt away.

At this time these sounds of the cracking are the beginnings of the crack in the ice that's built on nothing.

Nothing!

The waters of life flow freely without cost to anyone.

These other waters have become blocks of ice with no life in it.

Frozen.

Inactive and with no life in it.

So, the fire comes and works its works on these blocks of ice all over the world.

This fire, this HOLY GHOST and the fire of Pentecost that will not stop.

The fire will not stop doing its work in those places where freezing has taken place.

The fire is indiscriminate and simply melts away all the lifelessness, and the obstruction, and the blockade of it.

It's simply melted away and transformed into rivers.

Rivers of life, transformed by the fire.

Because of this process, this HOLY GHOST and the fire Pentecost process, and this propulsion, because of this, nothing will stop this HOLY GHOST and fire on the earth in men's hearts.

Melting the hardest ice block in a man's heart.

Melted by the fire.

Melted by the fire.

Many will go to heaven in this hour for it's HIS hour for this release in the Body of CHRIST.

Rejoice and be glad as you see the day approaching.

Looking past, beyond what you see, and looking unto JESUS, the author and the perfecter of this HOLY GHOST and fire.

"I will send another one just like ME."

This is the day of the sending of the HOLY GHOST and fire, Pentecost, and it will not behave or be reasonable, rational, or normal.

It cannot, cannot, cannot.

It's resurrection life, again, again, and again.

It will not be contained, or bound up, or controlled, or manipulated, or managed.

JESUS, it's your work. You do your work in your body and we hold fast to the HEAD in these days.

In this hour, we hold fast to the head, JESUS.

For it is GOD who is at work within us, both to will and to do of HIS good pleasure.

It is this day in the Body where YOU restore all the years the locust has eaten.

All the years, all the years YOU restore in a moment.

You restore because it's your timing, and your purposing, and your plan for your Body.

Eyes open, ears hearing, hearts perceiving.

Eyes seeing in the Name of Jesus.

CHAPTER 5
Gifts and Callings

5.1 I made you, so I know you

I chose you. You did not choose me but I chose you.
I made you.
I chose you to be who you are, how you are, every ability, how you look, how you breathe, how you talk, how you everything.
I chose you and made you who you are, so I know where you fit.

So, I know where you fit.

Everything that you are, every experience, every relationship, every part of your life, I put in place for you, for who you are now.
You do get to say, but you get to say within MY purpose, for I chose you and I know where you fit.
You walk in and it's true, you just fit.
You don't have to work at it to bring it about, or figure it out, for I know what I'M about.

It's a perfect fit.

5.2 This life under the radar

These gifts and callings are of HIS choosing.
They do not conform to the world's message and the world's methods of appointment.
They don't conform because they are eternal, and they are of HIS choosing.
They do not change and are not revoked.
They do not demonstrate or illustrate worldly giftings or abilities or achievements.

These giftings and callings of GOD are really under the radar.
They are hidden from the natural mind.
They're hidden because they cannot be obtained or grasped in any other way than by the SPIRIT.
They are indeed under the radar.
So that's why they're hidden in HIM. That's why they're in this hidden place.
These things are hidden in the heart and they are not accessible in any other way.
They cannot be received in any natural way.
They can't be understood or obtained any other way because they're under the radar.

They're hidden in the heart and from the mind, so they cannot be understood by or accessed in the mind.
Because these things are of the heart, they're of HIS kingdom that is not seen.
It's the unseen. It's the kingdom of the SON of HIS love which is under the radar.
It's under the covers, and so these things are hidden until the heart can speak these things into the head where the head can understand them in some fashion, but it's never in fullness, these things, never in fullness.

These things are a shadow of what the heart already knows, that's all it can ever be, just a representation of the reality that's already established in the heart.

It's the living out of the heart, it's the change of living out of the heart, not living out of the head.

And in the twinkling of an eye, on the way up, that change will be immediate and full and complete.

5.3 Life in the body

Because these gifts and callings never change, they are eternal, they never change.
They're filled with life, they are eternal.
They're from the Father so they are eternal.
These gifts and callings, they are eternal. They never stop. They are eternal.
Filled with life, they're filled with life.
Resurrection life. They are filled with Jesus.
He is the resurrection and the life.
They are filled with HIS life.

Life, life, life, where there's death, then there's life.
Bones filled with life. Bones filled with life.
Resurrection.
Resurrection.
All the gifts are filled with life, are filled with JESUS.
They are filled with HIS life.
All the gifts, all the callings are filled with JESUS.

No more dryness.
No more dry bones in the Body.
No more dry bones in the Body, because they are filled with life. The waters of life.
Lazarus, the coming forth, from death to life, from death to life. Filled with life.
His spirit in the Body, in the bones, resurrection life.
Flowing, and filling, and moisture, and the waters, waters, waters.

Thank you, LORD.

5.4 Demonstrating Jesus

So, you think you don't fit.
So, you think your life doesn't fit.
Love came in the person of JESUS CHRIST.
Grace came, took on flesh, and dwelt among men. Talk about not fitting.
Full of grace and truth.

However you try to fit in, it can never happen.
Fitting in can never happen because you're different. You're bought with a price.
This blood of the New Covenant says you're not your own. You're bought with a price.
Therefore, you glorify GOD in your body because you don't fit, and you can't fit, and you won't fit, every single time.
So, this whole life down here is about fitting in.
It's about how do you fit in so nobody notices who you really are.
So, you're under the radar.

You're bought with a price.
Therefore, you glorify GOD in your body because you're bought with a price.
The greatest price of all is the blood of this New Covenant that says YOU'RE my workmanship and I show you off.
I show you off to principalities and powers.
I demonstrate what I did in your body while you're here.
So, you cannot hide and fit in because you're hidden with CHRIST in GOD.
Because in HIM you live and move and have your being.
That's your place of hidden-ness and IN-ness.

Because of this reality, and because this is who you were made to be, you're HIS workmanship, created in CHRIST JESUS.
You are born anew that you would do those works and walk in those paths that HE has designed for you.

It displays HIM every time.

Every time it displays who HE is.

It demonstrates who HE is, therefore you get to say what you want, because it demonstrates who you are, and who HE is.

It's a demonstration of you being whoever HE needs you to be, living this abundant life.

Abundance of grace.

Free gift of righteousness.

Free everything in abundance.

That's why it never stops.

That's why it never shuts up.

That's why it never ceases, and it never diminishes.

It always increases, because HE's the GOD of more than enough all the time.

It demonstrates JESUS – every time!

CHAPTER 6
HIS Abundant Provision

6.1 Abundant life

I came to give you life, and that more abundantly.
Abundant provision in every area of your life.
I came to give you life. I did not come to give you fear. I did not come to give you torment.
I became the curse for you and took all the deserved punishment for any part of the curse.
I took all the punishment for not measuring up in the human state, becoming the curse in your stead.
I took it all and paid the price so you could be free of sin, sickness, poverty, and lack in this life for as long as you are here.
That's why I took on flesh so that you could be free HERE, and participate in MY life HERE.
I took on the debt that was required, and I took on the punishment that was required.
I took it on for your freedom.

You died with ME and rose with ME to this new existence. To this new life.
To this new creation, where all those old things are passed away and are become new.
Your very existence is new.
So, every time that old existence tries to speak to you, it is indeed a lie.
It is a lie because the price has already been paid for complete freedom from the tyranny of any curse.
All that which is motivated and propelled and exists through fear is from a spirit which you've NOT been given.
You have been given a spirit of POWER and love and a sound mind, which is constantly aware that "it is finished".
It is a constant reminder that there is no fear in HIS love.

So, this life is entirely different, where you rule and reign through one man, JESUS CHRIST.

You rule and reign with the authority given by the FATHER to the SON in you.

With that very same authority, as HE is, so are you in this world.

You get to rule and reign through one man JESUS CHRIST.

When you say what is already done in heaven, it comes to pass on the earth.

It comes to pass on earth because, in the authority with which you say that, it is already done and accomplished.

So you say to sickness GET OUT OF MY BODY.

You say to poverty GET OUT OF MY BANK ACCOUNT.

You say to trouble GET OUT OF MY FAMILY.

You say to strife GET OUT OF MY LIFE.

You say these things with the authority of JESUS within you because they are already accomplished.

There's no fear in HIS love.

HIS love that never changes.

HIS love never diminishes.

HIS love never stops.

Look at HIS love, at the quality and nature and character of HIS love, and there can be no fear.

As soon as you look outside that, it's like Peter walking on the water, and you sink, but as soon as you look into HIS love there is no fear.

Fear stops you from being who you are and from moving into the realm of HIS love.

Speaking the higher things from the higher place enables moving from that place of fear.

It enables you to move to the place in HIS love where there's actually no fear.

6.2 Waves of supply

This wave after wave, this inexorable supply, never stops.

It comes in wave after wave after wave after wave.

It never stops because the life is in these waters, in these waves, in this motion of it coming to you.

Wave after wave of supply of people, of places, of supply and supply.

It comes wave after wave just like the tides and just like the movement of the waters.

They come wave after wave, and there is nothing that stops them.

There is nothing that stops these waves of supply.

There's no activity that stops these waves of supply.

No thought that stops these waves of supply.

No word that stops these waves of supply.

This wave after wave of supply comes and flows and overflows every dry need, every need.

It's looking at this supply, the releasing of the supply, wave after wave after wave after wave.

No words stop it. No activity stops it. Nothing stops it.

HIS plan and HIS purpose will be fulfilled with this wave after wave after wave.

HIS plan and HIS purpose will overwhelm every need, and every place.

Overwhelming with HIS supply.

Boundless.

No boundary to HIS supply.

All the boundaries about anything are absolutely overwhelmed by the supply flowing in and washing away any boundary.

The limits of not here, not me, not now, not enough, or any boundary are washed away.

Just like the sound of music coming in waves.

Wave upon wave upon wave, crescendo, tempo, volume, wave after wave after wave.

That anointing.

That reality.

That life of GOD in the sound destroys any yoke of boundaries.

6.3 Overwhelming abundance

Look at the way that I do things.
When I do things, they are extravagant.
When I do things, they are always more than enough.
It's always more than you could even ask or think.
It's more than abundant.
It's more, all the time more.
It's increased more.
It's always more and more and more.

Every time you look at something you see the need, and the need for that need to be filled.
You see the need for that particular need to be filled, but I say I do the more and more.
I fill it up to overflowing, not just the particular need met.
Not just the particular vessel or need or circumstance met.
I pour out abundantly. Overflowing. So that there's always overflow.

It's always more than necessary.
I don't just do necessary, I do twelve baskets full left over after feeding thousands.
I don't just meet needs, **I overwhelm the need with MY life.**

I don't just make man feel better about himself, I give MYSELF to be his sacrifice for this new life.
It's abundant.
It's overflow.
It's more than enough.
It's not just, "Oh! It's OK, feel better," it's, "I give MYSELF so you don't even have to think about it."
I restore abundantly.

Look at this abundant life, and any need that you see.

Think about a fridge filled with food, filled and overfilled, that's how I do everything.

It's not just one little flower in the middle of a field, but a field of flowers, profuse, beautiful, and fragrant.

Everything assaulting senses with MY provision.

It's fragrant, loving, and overwhelming the senses with MY provision, not just a bandage on a sore or a hurt.

It's MY overwhelming new life abundantly poured into your very being.

This abundant life that I came to give you overflows its containing borders all the time.

It actually is Niagara Falls all the time, so just sit back and let me pour it out over every part of your life.

This IN HIM life, abundant life that's abundant, outrageous, and ostentatious.

I overwhelm the need with MY life.

6.4 The doors to HIS provision

JESUS is in charge of the doors.

HE opens doors and no man can shut the doors.

HE speaks to the doors and the doors open.

At the sound of HIS voice the doors open that have hitherto been closed and locked.

HE opens the doors for free flow, of going in and going out.

Man has nothing to say about these matters.

The doors are opened for HIS plan and purpose to be fulfilled, for the blood-bought believer.

There is no qualification for partaking of the supply.

Only blood! Only blood! Only blood!

The blood of JESUS is the security.

It's the place of it and the receiving of it and the living of it.

There is no other place, but to exist in it.

So just as Joseph gave bread to rescue his blood family, so JESUS is the bread for HIS blood family.

And with the blood of JESUS, the door is open.

Never locked, never shut, never excluding provision, and never shutting out.

The door never shuts out HIS blood-bought ones from HIM.

So eat and drink of HIM with abandon, with joy, with conviction, and with certainty.

Be in the place of security in HIM.

Eternally secure, for ever and ever.

6.5 Managing lack

All the managing of the lack in this realm.
It's all about the managing of the lack, of the "not enough" in any area.
How do I manage it?
How do I manage it?

And yet where the SPIRIT of the LORD is, there's liberty.
Liberty from all the managing.
"I have to manage it!"
"If I don't manage it, I'm WRONG."
"Shame on you, you didn't manage it!"
All the managing, the constant drip, drip, drip, of "it's up to you, you have to manage it" – whatever the "it" is.
And yet "it is finished".

Where the SPIRIT of the LORD is, there's liberty from the striving and the performance of managing all the time.
What happens if you don't manage it?
Then there's always hell to pay.
There's always the consequences of "shame on you".
And yet, where the SPIRIT of the LORD is, there's liberty!

The body of Christ is caught in the net of managing.
Caught in the net of it.
The whole world managing this life down here.
And how do I manage it?
And yet HE said, "It's finished, I've done it for you, be without a concern."

You're free of concern. Don't even think about it!
Shake the viper off, you don't have to manage it.
You don't have to manage the poison of the viper.

JESUS, flood the eyes of our heart with light so that we know the hope of this calling, the reality of this calling, that as YOU are, so are we in the world.

We believe it and we speak it, and IT IS DONE.

GLORY TO GOD!

6.6 The supply and the tyranny of self

You needed to be reconciled to the ONE who created you, so I came.
I came to be your supply.
I came to take your place.
I came to die your death.
I came to rise again, to be your resurrection.
I came to see you in me in the place of restoration of rulership.

It's all about the divesting of the Pharisaical clothing of:
"I can do it myself."
"I'll clothe myself."
"I'll be my own righteousness."
"I'll be my own supply."
"I'll be, I'll be."

It took resurrection life to set men free from that need to control, the tyranny of self.
As blood-bought ones we keep our eyes fixed on who HE is, and who we are in HIM.
Every time the gaze goes off HIM it's like being sucked back into that Pharisaical spirit of "I'm the supply and I know".
It took the life of GOD Himself, and the eternal and sacrificial blood of the LAMB, to do the job.
To do the "it is finished" job.

When we look outside the protection of the blood, and into that place of "Oh, now I have to be the supply", you're looking past HIM. There is no help in looking past HIM because HE's the place of safety and the covering of the blood and the "Oh, it's all done".
So, it's saying to yourself all the time, "It's done, it's already done."
Your time on this earth is for the constant living, moving, and having your being in the "it's already done".
So don't give credence to any other thought.
In heaven there is no other thought.

There's never any other thought.
It's divested of all the false covering, it falls off. It just falls off.
It has no power.
It has no voice.
It has nothing.
It's empty.
It's just filthy rags.

6.7 More than enough

You see a need in this realm and you want the need met.
In ME the need is already met.
Then you look at the need, and you see the need met.
You know the need is already met, but I say it's more than met.
It's not just met.
It's more than met.
It overflows the limits of the need.
It overflows the need.
It overwhelms the need.
It not only fills the need but it spills out everywhere around the need.
It doesn't just meet the need itself.

The blind man was healed.
Yes, he was healed but it doesn't stop there.
It impacts all those around, all those that see, all those that hear.
It doesn't stop there with the meeting of the need, because the meeting of the need spills out everywhere.
It spills out everywhere it goes, just like the twelve baskets full.
It's not just meeting the need that is merely stuck to down here.
Just meeting the need is stuck to limits of down here:
The limits of "this is the need, this is what I need, this is it".
And the limits of "I'll be satisfied when this particular need is met and I can check that off my list".
But in HIM there are no limits, and the need is more than met.
That's why it is such a display of the life in HIM.
Life in HIM is a demonstration.
It's more. It is the supernatural.
It's not just meeting the natural need.
It's not just making something better.
It's walking in the fullness, the overwhelming, the over spilling, the over abundant, the extravagant, and the outrageous.

It's not just paying off a debt, it's having money in the bank once the debt is paid.

It's not healing a spot on your body, it's walking in divine health all the time and knowing that you're free.

It's not just the particular need but it's the extravagant demonstration of this union of life IN HIM.

That's what this life IN HIM is.

You are fused with HIM. You are infused by HIM.

"He who is joined to the LORD is one Spirit with HIM."

This overwhelming, unreasonable, and irrational move of the HOLY GHOST and power is more than. Much more than.

We see it, we receive it, we eat of it, we drink of it, and partake of it, not only in the Communion but with our words.

We partake of it. We take it and speak it, and looking at YOU, we see it.

Today we receive the "more than", LORD.

And it's like a river flooding, not just a trickle of water coming down over the desert.

It's a flood coming into the desert and pushing out all the rocks that are in the way.

It's a flood that fills every crack, every hole, every crevice, every space with life.

It causes life, it brings forth life, so the desert blooms.

When the river floods there is a sound you hear before you see.

There is a sound, a rumble.

It builds and it builds, and then you see the beginnings of the flood, and then you see the flood. But the sound comes first.

In the upper room there was a sound.

The sound filled the room and spilled out of the windows to the people outside.

Then there was a flood, all over the earth!

CHAPTER 7
Life in the Spirit Realm

7.1 The sounds of the Spirit

This pouring out of the SPIRIT which cannot be contained is an offense to the flesh.
The thirst for the SPIRIT will not be satisfied by anything else.
That's why it's such an offense to the natural mind.

The sounds of it release the power, and stir up adversaries in the spirit realm.
The sound of the SPIRIT overwhelms and silences the ability of the adversary to permanently seduce the elect.
The blood of JESUS has opened and created the way for the reception of these HOLY SPIRIT sounds in the blood-bought heart.

This pouring out is the place of change, and of security.
It's the place of reality and demonstration of the life of the HOLY GHOST in the heart of man.

The eternal plan and purpose of GOD means that no one can remove from you the reality of CHRIST in you, the hope of glory.
GOD uses every step you take to see HIS plan and purpose released through you.

The sounds, the words that you speak from that place of knowing HIM, find an entrance in men's hearts.
Things that you speak from that place of knowing come to pass.
The words from that knowing place get released in HIS way at HIS time in the all-encompassing plan of the FATHER.

7.2 The sound of the SPIRIT

The sound of the SPIRIT overwhelms and overrides the sound of the whispers of the distractions of the enemy.
The sound of the SPIRIT overcomes the enemy that comes to say, "What about, what about . . ."
The sound of the SPIRIT overrides, overwhelms all those lying spirits.

It's like standing in, not beside, a waterfall, standing IN Niagara Falls where you lose your ability to process thoughts.
You lose your ability to process thoughts of "what does this mean, and what does that mean, and what is that saying."
You lose your ability to process all of those things.
They are overridden by the sound of the SPIRIT, by the rushing of the waters of the "it is finished, it is yours, it's finished, it's yours." Over and over and over again.

The washing of the water of the WORD, and the blood bought that washing.
The blood of JESUS bought that process, that living in that place of "it is finished".

7.3 The sound of "no limits"

There are never any limits to HIS love.
There are never any limits to HIS joy.
There are never any limits to HIS peace.
There are never any limits to HIS provision.
There are never any limits with GOD.

There is a sound of "there are no limits" because HE took the consequences of going beyond the limit.
There's some kind of consequence that is painful in some way, but in HIM there's no limit.
HE took all the consequences of pushing beyond the reasonable.
Beyond the rational.
HE took every consequence, every painful and bad consequence of pushing beyond what is reasonable.
HE took that into HIS body and carried it away so it's no longer part of our thinking or of our being IN HIM.

The sound of this moves into the realm that's different.
The sound of it moves into the realm of the unlimited.
That's why the sound is so quickening and so nourishing.
That's why the sound is so significant, because it moves you right into that place where you know there are no problems.
There are no problems because it's already done.
It's not just already done but it's actually yours to live in.

7.4 Speaking from within

The sound in the Spirit is an expression of the Spirit realm.
It's an expression of the realm of the heart.
The sound comes out as an expression of the breath of the SPIRIT.
GOD breathed life.
HE spoke, "Light be!" And it was.

The force of the breath of GOD releases life into a situation and alters the situation.
The very sound of the breath of GOD releases life into the situation.

The breath comes from the Spirit within.
The sound is carried on the breath.
The heart is bought with the blood of JESUS.
When the heart believes, the Spirit speaks and gives voice to that which is within.

The words that are spoken demonstrate the existence of the SAVIOUR within.
When the blood of JESUS is declared, as protection and provision, the act of speaking it fills the situation with HIS life.
When HIS blood is declared it fills the situation with HIS life and goes and does what has been spoken.

The power of the life of GOD within the blood-bought believer causes those words to come to pass.
They attract HIS provision and the supply.
They manifest and demonstrate the source.
They come from the reality, the substance of the Spirit within.

It does not require an understanding of that speaking to speak.
All it requires is what is known in the heart.
It's the place of knowing, not understanding.

Even without understanding, everything necessary is drawn to those words because they emanate from the SPIRIT within.

The words come from the SPIRIT of GOD resident within the human being, the blood-bought human spirit.
They come from the place of fusion of the two, being one spirit with HIM.

The needed supply is irrevocably drawn and stuck to those words with one purpose to demonstrate who the SAVIOUR is.
Who JESUS is.

7.5 The IN HIM place

Every time you come to this place, this place is here for you.
Every time you give yourself to this place, it is here for you.
Every time you partake of this, every time you eat of this, every time you drink of this, it is here for you,
Every time, it is here for your edification, your building up.
Every time it is for the stirring up of that gift of God that is within you, that has been placed in you, it is there all the time.
There's free access to that place.
There's always freedom of access.
There's never any withholding – ever!

It is simply a question of "yes", it's always "yes", and it's always now because it is there – always!
It's always there.
It's always there, because in fact it is your life.
It's where you live, and you move, and you have your being.
It's where your being is.
It's in this place, and from this place, and through this place, that is always there.
It's a simple thing.
It's as simple as breathing.
It's as present as breathing.
So, this place of joy.
This place of fulfillment.
This place of satisfaction is always, always, always a breath away.

It's the place of peace.
It's the place of knowing.
It's the place of power.
It's the place of the blood where power flows unrestrained and unrestricted by any other thought.

It's as simple as breathing.

7.6 Cause and effect

He whom the SON sets free is free, therefore you're not bound to be like anyone else.
There's no more, "Oh, you're bound to be like someone in your family, you're bound to be."
The natural course of events binds you to be and do something.
The natural course of events binds you to that cause and to that effect.
You're bound to that in the natural.
But he whom the SON sets free is free indeed, and there's no more binding.

You're not bound to be like your natural parents.
You're not bound to be like your natural father, because you have your FATHER in heaven.
You're a child of the FATHER of heaven, and you're HIS progeny.
Your DNA in the natural says you're bound to be.
The natural says cause and effect.
The supernatural supersedes and overrules the natural.

Everything in the natural is cause and effect.
There's a binding in the natural.
There's a constriction.
There's a limiting.
There's a constraining.
There's an, "Oh well, it's only natural this would happen because of that, it's only natural."
Of course it's natural. Of course it's reasonable.
This happens, so then that will happen, as a natural course of events.

But in the supernatural this does NOT apply, because 'in HIM' you live and you move.
In HIM you go from one place to another.
You go on paths that HE's directed.
You follow what HE's put in your heart when HE said, "What is that to you if one lives or one dies, what is that to you?"

"What is that to you because you follow ME."

The leading of the SPIRIT within guides, and teaches, and instructs, and comforts, and strengthens, and renews, and quickens.

The leading of the SPIRIT does all the work that is necessary for this life and godliness.

Everything comes from within, from the "in HIM" place, so the cause and effect is no longer operative.

Cause and effect has no more to say about your life here.

So, every time you look at cause and effect, you exalt its ability to regulate or determine.

Cause and effect is actually a red herring.

It's a distraction.

It's a lie.

It's an actual lie.

Cause and effect, with all the measuring, all the counting, all the determining, has nothing to do with:

"In HIM you live and move and have your being," and

"He whom the SON sets free is free."

That's why Lazarus was given as such a picture of cause and effect, it has nothing to do with life IN HIM, nothing.

7.7 Time and the two realms

In this realm, it feels like you are waiting.
In this realm, everything changes on a dime, everything changes in the twinkling of an eye.
Time is the regulator.
Time is the determiner.
Time is the thing that regulates what happens.
So everything feels like waiting, because that what time does.
Time operates in the laws that are down here, through the understanding, the looking, the gauging, and the perceiving.

But your life is in HIM, so time really has no regulatory force in your life.
HIS plan and HIS purpose does, but time does not.
Plan and purpose is from the higher place.

You are created in CHRIST JESUS, HIS workmanship.
You were born in HIM that you would walk in the paths that HE's prepared.
Living the good life that HE prepared.
It feels like waiting, but it's not actually waiting.

Everything that's seen in this realm is coloured by time.
Coloured by the things that are in place in this realm.
But you're not solely of this realm.
You are born of the Spirit, from above.
Created to live and move and have your being in the Spirit.
Just your physical being is of this realm.

You are a supernatural being living in a natural realm.
He created us to live in both realms simultaneously, the timeless supernatural put into the natural time-ruled realm.
That which is outside time, inserted into time, co-existent.

HE brings to you all the things that are necessary for this natural realm. HE has already established those things in the supernatural realm, in which you are "in HIM", where you live and move and have your being.

Our life is about looking at the interaction of the two realms, where we exist while we're here.

It's looking at it differently.

Seeing it differently through different eyes.

The eyes of your heart actually know things your head cannot grapple with.

THAT is that place of joy and peace.

7.8 The SPIRIT does not conform to the earthly

The things that are of the SPIRIT come from the FATHER of light.
The divine things come from the FATHER of light.
The deep things come from the FATHER of light.
The things that are born of the SPIRIT are energized and come from the FATHER of light.

These things that are of the SPIRIT do not conform to the things of the flesh.
They do not conform to the earthly.
They do not conform because they cannot conform.
They will not conform.

These things are eternal in origin.
Eternal in nature.
Eternal in expression.
And when they take on flesh in the natural realm, they simply will not be managed.

There was nothing in the water pots.
There was not even water in the water pots at Cana of Galilee, but as soon as Love was manifested the need was met.
Even now, the Person of love comes and everything pours out from there.

You receive these things by the SPIRIT but the mind of the flesh rails against it because it cannot receive the things of GOD.
The mind of the flesh is at enmity, set against the things of GOD.
The things that measure, and feel, and touch, and all the sense things are at enmity to the "it is finished, it is done, and here it is".

When the day of Pentecost was fully come, the HOLY SPIRIT came with a sound.
When all the circumstances and people and provision had fully come, then the HOLY SPIRIT came as the sound.

Pentecost is the now time.

It is the fully come.

The fullness of it has come.

The readiness is released in the SPIRIT and the "fully come" becomes reality, and then everything is immediately in place.

CHAPTER 8
Earthly Realm versus Spirit Realm

8.1 SPIRIT versus flesh

It's this business of attempting to make, and to force the things of the SPIRIT to behave like things of the flesh.

It's this propensity, this drive, this demand, that the things of the SPIRIT must behave like the things of the flesh.

It absolutely cannot be because they are two different realms.

They are oil and water.

They cannot agree.

The flesh will not submit to the "it is finished, I've got it covered".

The flesh will never shut up, because every time the spirit of fear rises up, it fuels the flesh.

It's like fuel.

It fuels the flesh, that spirit of fear.

That spirit fuels the flesh to a place of prominence and dominance.

Every time you come up against that thing, it's actually a spirit.

It's not behaviour.

It's not a personality.

It's not like a personal quirk.

It's not someone just saying 'well that's the way they are'.

Well NO, it's a spirit that drives it and compels one to behave a particular way.

It behaves the same way it did when JESUS walked the earth.

It wants dominance.

It wants attention.

It says, '"Look at me. Listen to me. I'm right. I know. You'd better . . . and if you don't . . ."

It's the seduction of the flesh to be in charge.

It's the flesh who says what it should be.

It's the flesh who says how it should be done.

It's the flesh who says who should do it.

It's the flesh who says when it should be done.

The flesh wants to dominate.

It wants to be exalted and to be in charge.

But the blood-bought believer actually has the life of GOD inside to say, "NO, shut up, go away, discussion over."

There is no talking to it.

There is no engaging in debate.

There's no tolerance for it in the blood-bought believer.

There's no tolerance for the seduction of the flesh.

It constantly comes and says, "Did GOD really say? I know better."

But the blood of JESUS repels that lie that comes to seduce away from the reality of "I've got it covered", and the blood is the final word on it.

That's why you overcome with the blood of the Lamb and the word of your testimony.

It's covered. JESUS' blood covers it, and that's the truth.

That's what this life is.

That's what the whole of this life, past, present, and future, is.

The blood of JESUS covers all things, the whole existence.

8.2 The work of the supernatural

In the WORD all the supernatural is actually SUPER-natural.

The supernatural is above the natural.

It's where you walk on water.

It's that which is not possible in the natural, it's above the natural.

The man whose eyes were healed with spittle in the dust, that's supernatural.

It's taking the natural and elevating it in the SPIRIT realm to accomplish that which the natural cannot do.

This elevation, this lifting up of the thoughts, enables one to receive what's already been done.

The natural thoughts keep the attention stuck to the earth where there is no help.

There is simply a magnifying of any natural symptom.

All that the earth can do is magnify the symptom and give it more power.

All that the earth can do is give it more influence.

All that the earth can do is give it more place.

The natural symptom wants to be thought of all the time, but it is just a viper to be shaken off and thrown back into the fire.

That's why there's no permanent solution to looking at the symptom.

The body is designed to heal itself.

It is a supernatural plan built into the natural human body to enable it to restore and renew itself through rest.

But the constant looking and figuring out of the symptoms is not a state of rest, it is the opposite, and it's a state of torment.

But HE came to set men free from every work of the enemy.

The SON of GOD was manifested to destroy every work of the devil.

HIS peace drives the torment out.

HIS peace sweeps it away.

HE sweeps the fear and torment away.

As soon as Peter looked at JESUS he was able to do the supernatural. Even before the cross, the power of looking was so great.

The power of seeing is so great that the natural is changed by the supernatural with the looking.

8.3 Living our life down here

Life IN HIM does not look like or conform to anything in this realm down here.

Things of this realm want to be accumulated.

Everything in this realm, in the earthly, wants to be stuck, attached to the earth.

Everything seen is always within this earthly attachment and is subject to change.

But our life is IN HIM and originates from above because we are seated with HIM above all principalities, powers, and rulers of wickedness in high places. You're seated with HIM above that.

You're seated looking down, ruling and reigning through one man, JESUS CHRIST, because of the blood of this New Covenant.

You're not stuck to the earth and the way things work down here.

You're not controlled, or regulated, or constrained, or constricted, or tied to this earthly realm.

You're here just for a time, and yourself IN HIM is not of this realm. It's not stuck to the earthly.

You are not subject or enslaved to the earthly way because HIS way is always higher, above, overwhelming, and overruling.

HIS way overrules the "down here" every time, so, live and move and have your being IN HIM.

It's about the letting go of the attachment of being stuck to the way it is down here.

Letting go of the way it works, and letting go of all the laws in place down here.

Those things lose their ability to regulate and determine your life because your life is otherwise.

This blood has set you apart IN HIM to live a life that lets go of the old life down here.

The down here has no power to regulate or determine your life, ever, because HE does it in ways that are not regulated or determined by down here. It's always higher and otherwise.

The whole of life down here is running after resources, running after supply, running after a constant "how do I get it done?"

"Do I have enough?"

"Is there enough?"

"Where do I get enough?"

"How do I fill the need?"

"How do I meet the need?"

"How do I? How do I? How do I?"

It's constant. It's the stuff of life down here, in the earthly.

It's a constant condition of life down here, but your life is IN HIM, where HE says, "I've already done it, the blood has already accomplished it and it is finished."

You are covered, it's done, and you don't have to think about it because it's already done, and you don't have to be anxious.

You don't have to be fearful, you don't have to be running after, you don't have to be looking at it all the time.

Just say, "Thank you, LORD, it's done," and so it's done, and the blood is the stamp on it.

The blood is the "paid in full" about all the running around.

The whole earth is running around trying to get their needs met, but HE said, "I came so you are free of that constant drive and lust that never shuts up, so I shut it up with my blood. I shut that down."

8.4 Freedom from encumbrances

HE made you to be free.
Filled with HIM.
Free from any limitations of your thoughts about yourself.

That is what HE has done with the body and the blood.
It is true.
HE whom the SON sets free is free indeed.

Imagine yourself free from any limitation or encumbrance.
HE has bought your freedom with HIS blood, so you can look at that freedom and imagine yourself walking through this life free of any bondage or limitation.
Filled with joy.
Filled with peace.
Filled with power.
All because HE lives in you.
See yourself IN HIM.

All things are possible with GOD.

He whom the SON sets free, is free indeed.
You are bought with the body and the blood of JESUS CHRIST.
It has been paid for in full.
It is finished.
HE took all the limitation into HIMSELF – SO YOU DON'T HAVE IT!

So try it now.

8.5 HE is the GOD who changes things

Everything in this earthly realm is subject to change.
There is nothing fixed, nothing to be relied upon.
They can be changed, and are changed by the ONE who changes things.
Changed by HE who is the great I AM.
Changed by HE who says, "This is the way it is."

HE is the ONE who alters circumstances.
HE is the ONE who supersedes natural laws.
HE is the ONE who transforms people.
In this earthly realm everything is subject to change, and is changed by HE who changes things.

You can't trust the evidence of your natural eyes.
You can't trust what you see as physical evidence before you.
It will look like one thing one moment, and the next moment it will be something else.
You cannot trust the evidence of your eyes.
You cannot trust it, but you can trust the ONE who changes things.

In HIS Spirit realm, where we live and move and have our being, things are fixed.
In the earthly realm circumstances are changed by HIS word to demonstrate HIM.
It's the flow of HIS life in us and through us that brings about these changes.
So, the things that we see are changed by HIM.
The things that we hear are changed by HIM.
The things that we touch are changed by HIM.
The things that we think about are changed because of HIS life flowing in us.
HIS life in us gives us the right to speak HIS word that changes the things of the natural realm.

8.6 The big lie of the flesh

This is the place of rest where I've done it all.
It's the only place of rest.
It's the only place of peace.
It's the only place of joy where I've done it all.

It is in such opposition to the lust of the flesh to do the doing.
It is in such opposition to the flesh that says, "I know how to achieve rest."
It is in such opposition to the flesh that says, "I know how to achieve joy."
It is in such opposition to the flesh that says, "I know how to achieve peace, I'm the answer."
It is in such direct opposition to the lust and to the drive of the flesh to be the answer.

My Spirit within is the well to draw from.
Draw from the well of life within.
Drink of living water.
Eat the bread of life that satisfies.
Drink of the life in the blood that redeems and repels that insatiable lust that wants to be the answer.
Draw from the wells that are within, even without the understanding of it. The capacity to draw from it is simple, so simple.
The flesh wants to make it complicated and so difficult that you can't even grasp it, but the reality is on the inside, in Him.
The outside says, "I'll change, and that changes everything inside" – but it's the opposite!
He changes the outside from the inside.

It's the opposite to what it looks like.
That's why the flooding of the eyes of the heart with light brings understanding, for with the heart man believes.
It's the "yes" of the heart that floods out and affects the exterior.

That affects the wrapping of the earthen vessel.
It's by the supernatural.
It's by the spiritual.

That's why the inside actually wins all the time because it's GOD inside.
That's why the LORD floods the eyes of our heart with light so that we know the hope of HIS calling.
The reality is: In YOU we live and move and have our being.
That's why the anointing inside, the reality of HIM in us, destroys yokes of bondage every time, so you don't fall for it.

8.7 Remember who you are

Remember who you are.
Remember the price that was paid so you can be who you are.
Remember the price that was paid so you can be who you were created to be.
Every time that you look at yourself through the filter of looking at yourself, through yourself, you will stumble.
You are bound to stumble because this is the realm where it's normal to be bound.
You're bound to limitation.
You are bound to fear.
You are bound to every part of the curse.
You're bound to that.
So, every time you look at yourself through that, you're bound.

Look at yourself through what HE created you to be.
Where you live in HIM, and move, and have your being.
The place where there's no limit. Ever.
Every time you look at the limitation, you're limited.
Every single time you're bound to be limited, because you're looking from that realm of being bound, of bondage.
You are limited to being tied up, to not enough, to "no it can't, it's impossible".
But you're actually created to be in a different place where there's no limitation.
A place where there's no limitation.
A place where there's no bondage.
A place where there's not any of that.

This place of no limitation IN HIM, is looking at yourself through HIM because you are yourself IN HIM.
Just as HE is, so are you in the world.
So, there's actually no limit.
Start to look at things in your life through the glasses of "no limit". Ever.

That is a complete change.

With men it's always impossible but with GOD it's never impossible.

It's always possible.

It's not just possible, it's done.

It's who HE made you to be in this life, and it never makes sense.

There is a thrust to push the limits out of the way for the things that are limiting.

This thrust is a propellant to "get out of my way!"

The limitation speaks of containment.

It speaks of smallness.

It speaks of not enough.

It speaks of this realm and it's not where you are created to live from.

The word inside us is working all the time against all the destruction that has come because of the curse.

It's a constant changing and restoring and renewing and rebuilding and renovating, and it never stops.

It's always renewing and quickening our very bodies to be what HE's already paid for.

It's what HE does in HIS blood-bought ones all the time.

It's what HIS body and blood constantly does, never stops.

It's all the time, always working, always perfecting that which HE started in the beginning.

Your freedom IN HIM.

8.8 It's new every day

This is a new covenant.
I've made a new creation.
I'm doing a new thing.
It's always new, every day is new.
It's not like yesterday.
SO STOP IT!

Stop looking at yesterday, the way it was, and the way it behaved and appeared to be, and the way it seemed to be, yesterday.
Looking at it, and looking at it, and looking at what it was like yesterday.
Stop it, don't do it, there's no life in it because it's new.
Every day is new.
Remember the manna in the wilderness, you couldn't keep it till the next day, it went rotten.
So the stuff of yesterday is done, and today is new and it's filled with life, and it's filled with the promise of this day.

Watch ME do stuff you've never seen before.
I do not repeat myself.
I made you a new creation in CHRIST.
I made you new, so you are new today.
There are new ways of looking at yourself, of thinking about yourself.
It's a New Covenant.
Not experienced before.
Never seen before.
Never heard of before.
Never done before.
Never thought of before.
Because I do things from above where there's nothing comparable about what's above and down below.
They're different realms, and they behave differently, and they demonstrate different things, and never the twain shall meet.
So it's new.

Just because something behaved in a particular way yesterday, last night, 20 minutes ago, does not mean it's about to behave that way again because MY life inside you is new.

You're not bound to react to whatever symptom of this realm in the way that you did before, because I do a new thing and my life brings fresh energy, power, and new life to every particle of who you are.

CHAPTER 9
Moving into the Spirit Realm

9.1 Moving from the natural to the supernatural

Moving from the natural to the supernatural is like moving out.
It's the moving out of the natural constrictions and confinements.
It's the not seeing yourself in those constrictions.
It's the not seeing yourself in the smallness of it.
It's the not seeing yourself in the containment of it.
It's moving out of that.
It's the moving out of looking at that.
It's the moving out of seeing oneself in that.
It's the moving out of that.

Once that's seen in the heart and spoken out, there's a moving out.
And that is done not by might nor by power but by my SPIRIT, says the LORD.
It's a moving out of it.
Once that's received in the way that HE does it, looking at it in the way that HE looks at it, then it finds expression that bursts the constriction.
That's why it can't be contained in a building.
It can't be contained.
Just as surely as the gifting and calling of GOD cannot be contained.

Today, FATHER, in the name of JESUS, we speak to the containment of it to open up!
Containment no longer has a place to constrict and limit the gifting and the calling of GOD.
We are free, without constriction.

9.2 Stepping out

This place right now is the stepping out, onto the water.

It's the releasing of yourself to the stepping on to that which will not hold you or support you.

It's a releasing of your control of it.

It's a releasing of your control of the thinking.

It's a releasing of your control of the constant ruminating.

It's constant, over and over and over, to make it come into some kind of order.

But the things of God will not come into any kind of order.

Speak to all that ruminating in the name of JESUS.

Bring it down in the name of JESUS, and speak release to your heart.

Walk by your heart.

See by your heart.

Hear by your heart those things that you do know.

You know them because they are established.

Those things are in you and they're part of you.

They're actually you, but the other isn't you.

In the name of JESUS all of it falls off.

All of the reasonings fall off you.

They're dead works.

That's not who you are any more.

Those works can no longer try to inform you or show you who you are.

You are cut off from them.

You are free.

JESUS has made you free.

Now you start to see by the eyes of your heart and you move into your freedom, and live and rejoice in it.

9.3 Deep wells

The dryness demands watering.
The intrinsic life of JESUS in the believer draws the water from the wells of salvation.
The existence of the water, in and of itself, has a sound that speaks to the heart.
It says to the heart, come and drink.
It says to men and women, go deep in the well, to the refreshing water that comes from the deep place in GOD.
The rushing of the deep water.

We've had enough of the shallow water.
It's too easy to go in and out of the shallow water.
We have exhausted it.
But you can drink of the deep water.

The deep water is like light coming into the dark places, coming up into the day.
We speak to the Body of CHRIST to come to the place of drinking where you lay aside your luggage.
Lay aside your weapons.
Look deep into the wells.
Put your head into the well.
Such a drink!
Drink deeply.
There's no other taste.
Nothing else can satisfy.
The shallow waters don't satisfy, only the deep waters can satisfy your spirit and your body.
Only the deep waters satisfy.
We drink it before we know it.
We drink it by faith, and when we drink it, we know it.

FATHER, send shepherds to lead the sheep into this place and into this drink.

Shepherds to lead the way to the fountain of living water, where the DNA of GOD is complete in you.

9.4 Music and Worship 1

Worship moves the music, the sound, up from the earthly, from being on the ground.
It moves up the natural notes and the natural sound into the realm of the Spirit.
As soon as that happens the expectation of the heart changes, to see answers coming from that place.
The release of the sound of that anointing changes the reception of it.
It is not from the place of experience.
It is not from the place on the ground.

It is not from the expectation of the ground.
It moves it up to the expectation of the SPIRIT, where the life is.
That's the place of the life.
That's the "IN HIM you live".
That's where your life comes from.
That's where the life in the blood comes from.
It's that place.
That's where the life in the blood flows to the highest mountain and deals with it.
That's where the life in the blood flows to the lowest valley.
From that place it flows down to it and it deals with it, and it covers it.

It's not tied to the earth with bonds of the earth.
Not tied to the place of "it's impossible".

It moves up.
To the answers.
To the release.
To the untying.
To the cutting of the bondages.
To the higher place.
To the place of the anointing.

There's no difference between a mountain too high and a valley too low, in that place.

It doesn't make any difference because the blood goes and deals with the situation.

It's already dealt with.

It's where the expectation comes from.

It's in that place.

The blood moves out of the supernatural and moves into the natural realm to accomplish those things in the natural that could not be done by the natural.

So our expectation comes from there, and we give thanks to you, LORD.

We receive it from that place into this place as done and finished because the blood always says "it is finished".

9.5 Music and Worship 2

In the process of making music, and particularly in making music as worship, you forget about yourself.
In the process of worship you forget about what makes sense.
You forget how you bring this SPIRIT of worship into the sense realm.
You forget how you bring it down to sensible, to the reasonable, to the understandable, and to a workable activity.
You forget about that because you give yourself to the production of the sound.
It comes from your heart.
It goes into your fingers.

It releases this platform for you.
It's like a jetty that goes out on to the water where you can't go from your head.
You can't walk on the water in your head.
It's impossible.
But you can walk on water because it's your jetty, it's a jetty.
It's a platform, it's a place, it's a way.

You can't participate in your head, on the water.
You can't do it because your head resists with every bit of the strength of head knowledge.
When you force it into being reasonable and understandable, it stops the flow.
With this force of bringing it into order, it stops the flow.
With this force of bringing it into reason, it stops the flow.
It's the impediment to the heart and the sound.
Giving yourself to the sound is your ease of it.
It gives you a way to do that which you cannot do.

You forget about yourself.

9.6 Receiving the things of GOD

HE came and manifested himself as a rushing mighty wind on the day of Pentecost.
It had nothing to do with the people, they were just standing there.
People were gathered together, expecting HIM in some way, but HE came in a way that was unexpected.
They did not expect tongues of fire to sit over each head.
They did not expect the sound of a rushing mighty wind to come in and fill the place where they were gathered.
They did not expect that.
They were just gathered, in some way expecting something, but didn't know what it was.

The HOLY SPIRIT came and filled their senses with the sound of the wind, and with the sight of the tongues of fire over each head.
These things may have seemed to be metaphors, they were in fact physical reality.
Tongues of fire over the heads to be seen, to be seen by their senses.
The HOLY SPIRIT coming in and filling the place as a rushing mighty wind.
To be heard, to be heard by their senses.

For HE who made the winds and the fire, and everything that is, this is not a problem.
That's why the blood is such an affront.
How can you speak of the blood and sing of the blood and expect things to change?
How can you do that?
How can you expect that?
Because HE who created everything shed the blood and said, "it is finished."
Body broken.
Blood shed.
It is finished.

The mind cannot receive the things of GOD.

In fact, the mind will not submit to any of the blowing winds and tongues of fire.

This is indeed why there is that prayer in Ephesians 1:18.

"LORD, flood the eyes of our heart with light so that we know," is for the body of CHRIST in these days. Flooding the eyes of the heart with light so you can know the reality of this calling, the reality of this life. This calling where "you have not chosen ME but I chose you."

I chose you for it, so I do all that is necessary for you to walk in this place where your head cannot receive the things of GOD.

Only the eyes of your heart can look at these things and know they are real.

9.7 Suddenly, everything changes

I do the "suddenly".
I do the "suddenly".
With ME, situations turn on a dime.
Situations and circumstances turn on a dime with ME.
I provide remarkable "suddenlies".

It's because of the time that suddenly it's time.
It wasn't time ten minutes before, and suddenly it's time.
Because of the time, suddenly it is time.
It might seem the preparation took a long time, but the manifestation is suddenly on time.
The demonstration in the natural is suddenly on time.
Suddenly!
Suddenly everything changes.

Try it now!
TRY it now!
Try IT now!
Try it NOW!

Suddenly everything changes.
In a moment.
Everything changes in that moment of revelation.
Everything changes in that moment of demonstration.
In that moment of "everything changes", it's all changed.
In a moment, in the twinkling of an eye, all changed.
Direction changed.
Circumstances changed.
Provision changed.
Everything changed.

Changed!
Changed!
Changed!

It's like the ratcheting of cogs in a wheel that are out of alignment and that suddenly fit into place.

They fit into place, they just fit into place. It's a suddenly, "Oh! Now it's clicked into place and there you go."

And there you go!

It's a pattern.

It's a pattern of the working of revelation.

Revelation is a "suddenly".

Everything changes the moment revelation hits.

Everything's changed.

It's all completely different.

Everything has just suddenly clicked into place and then that's IT!

9.8 Praise – The Answer

PRAISE is the access point of release from the prison of self-obsession.
From the tyranny of self.
It's a prison, it's tyrannical, and it won't let you go.
PRAISE releases, just like as in Acts where PRAISE opened the prison doors and was the release from the prison.
PRAISE moves it off and opens the door so you can see who you really are.
So you can come out and see who you really are.
Who you actually are.
Just as Peter came to himself with his miraculous deliverance from the prison.

There really is no other way because the mind of the flesh always wants pre-eminence.
It will never shut up, and that's why praise is the only way out.
It's a change of focus, a change of energies.
The exertion of the energy of the person, where the energy and all the focus and activity is off the self and onto HIM.

And then you're free.

CHAPTER 10
Seated Above in the Higher Place

10.1 The higher place

So, this place that I've set you in is a higher place.
I've seated you in a heavenly place beside me and in me.
This is the place that I have seated you in.
I have placed you in this place to operate from and to speak from.
This is the vantage point that you speak from.
My words are the words that you speak and they are higher words.
These words that you speak do not conform, nor are they regulated to down here.
These words are not regulated to the place that is transitory and subject to constant change.

The place that I've seated you in is a high place.
That's why you're drawn to high places and to looking at life from that higher place.
That's why every time you look from the low place you are subject to those things that are in the low place.
But you are not created to function out of the low place.
Instead, you are here for just a short time to occupy a place on the earth.
In that low place.
But the high place is where you're drawn to.
This high place soars above, operating with the eyes of above and not with the eyes of below.
The eyes of below bring such fear about anything and everything.
But looking from above, from the place where you are created for, is empowering.
So, every time you speak from the high place, power flows into the lower place.
Every time you speak from the higher place, it changes the lower place to conform to the higher place.
So, every time you speak the "it is finished", the "it is done, and it's yours", it changes the things that are down in the lower place.
This lower place, the earthly place, is where there is constriction, and constraint, and smallness, and poverty.

That's why this earthly place is so abhorrent and that's why you run from it every time you look at it.

You run from it and you run to the higher place.
You run to the "Oh, it's finished, it's done, that's not who I am", and you run because of who you are, every single time.
You are drawn to this higher place because that sense of rulership comes from there.
There is a physicality to it, and an expanse to it.
It's a place where you're not bound by the smallness of the earth.
That's why there's such a drawing to the higher things.
That's why the lower stuff falls off like dead leaves.
It's of no interest and it loses its ability to seduce.

The higher things are so empowering.
You rule and reign through one man CHRIST JESUS because of the blood in that higher place.
The anointing destroys yokes of bondage, because the anointing is from the higher place.
That is the very essence of the higher, of the being in HIM, where you live and move and have your being.
With rulership comes authority because as HE is, so are you in the world, to call into being those things that are not as if they are.
In that moment of speaking those things, the empowerment of the resurrection life fills and quickens your physical body.
That same spirit that raised CHRIST from the dead quickens your mortal body while you're here, when you speak those things.
And it's done, and you know it's done when you speak those things.

This place is the place of joy and the place of power.
It's the place of knowing and the place of receiving.
It's the place of "in HIM you live and move and have your being", where HE created you just like HIM.
So, you speak these things from the higher place.
You speak these things that are impossible from the lower place, and you

speak them as though they are, and they are.

This speaking from the higher place is a prophetic thing.

It is a prophetic thing that gives reality to the things which are not.

It gives reality to them by the words.

The words bring reality and the words create reality.

So the word that is spoken is covered.

Flesh comes on that word that is spoken, reality comes on that word.

JESUS was the word and HE became flesh.

JESUS took on flesh, so the word that is spoken from the higher place takes on flesh.

Words take on reality in this earthly realm, this lower place.

You say, "I'm going and the LORD's going to provide."

Speak it and you just walk into it and it happens because it's the life of GOD inside.

So, JESUS in you, speaks in and through you.

So, your words are filled with the empowerment of the "taking on flesh".

It's about taking on reality in this lower realm, from the higher realm.

So that's why words are filled with power.

So as you speak it, it takes on flesh.

It takes on materiality in this realm.

It takes on flesh at the perfect time and it's opened up to you so you start to walk in this thing.

When you walk in this thing it gets bigger, it increases and expands.

It's fuller and it fills all those places where it's needed.

So, it's different, and it does actually destroy yokes of bondage, every time it comes out of your mouth it takes on flesh.

Every time it comes out of your mouth, it takes on material existence.

It takes on reality.

It really is speaking things from the place above, that are not as though they are.

The evidence says it this way, but I say it's the opposite.

Every time you look at how it looks here, the evidence is contrary, is contrary to what I say about it.

What I say about it is in exact opposition and batters away at the physical, at the natural, and at the limited evidence down here.

There are limits to everything down here, that's the way it is.

That is the reality down here.

Down here is always limited resources.

It can only go so far and then there's no more.

But I say it's unlimited and you speak from that place just as I do.

You say this man (as in Acts 3), through and by the name of JESUS, is made sound in body now, before your eyes.

Soundness and completeness, that's what I say from the place where I've put you to speak.

I put you in a high place to speak those things which are not as though they actually are.

They are changed in the moment of the speaking from that place.

That high place is in direct opposition to the evidence of your eyes in this lower place.

It's in direct opposition.

In this life where you hold these two polar opposites in relationship to each other, you cannot trust in the evidence of your eyes, but you can trust in the evidence of your heart.

The heart reality supersedes and rules over the natural course of events and how things work.

The heart speaks that which the mind cannot bring into a reasonable sequence of events.

The sequence of events has no more rulership over the heart reality.

That's why you say what's in your heart and it comes to pass, because it overrules the natural way of doing things.

10.2 The place of joy and peace and supply

There is a place above.
It's the place where there's peace.
It's the place where there's power.
It's the place where there's anointing.
It's the place where you are created to live and move and have your being in HIM.
It's the place of exaltation of HIM, of lifting up HIM, and what HE's done, and the "it is finished".
It's the place where the blood always speaks of victory and the body always speaks of wholeness for you.
That place is the place to speak from about anything.
Every time you speak of what it is down here, there's no peace, there's no joy, and there's no supply.
But speaking from that place above, there's always joy and peace and supply.
Always. Always. Always.

This life in HIM is keeping your eyes and your gaze on the things that are unseen.
This is the place of calling into being those things which are not as though they are.
This is the place of joy and peace and supply.
Every time you speak from the higher place where joy and peace and supply are, you speak those things into material existence.
That's why there's no benefit in speaking about the "down here".
There is no benefit in giving it a voice.
There's no peace in it.
There's no joy in it.
There's no supply in it.

You died with HIM.
You rose with HIM.
You're seated with HIM in heavenly places in CHRIST JESUS.

Resident within you is the purposing of GOD to enable you to understand that you are like HIM.

You are like HIM while you have this physical existence on earth.

Everything is "in HIM", and so the speaking of the "in HIM" is the reality of your existence.

Therefore, say "it is done" because it is done, and then there's joy and there's peace and there's supply.

All the gifts and all the abilities and all the experiences of your life are the equipment.

Just as surely as a soldier is equipped with everything he needs to do his job, you too are equipped.

Just as surely as a surgeon is equipped with everything he needs to do his job, so anyone, he or she, is equipped for the job.

You are equipped in HIM for the assignment, for the purposing HE has for you.

It actually is nothing to do with you as the generator of any of the gifts, talents, abilities, opportunities, or experiences.

It's all from above and so there is no boasting in it.

The gifts and the talents are resident within your physical body.

You did not choose them.

You did not generate them.

So you cannot say, "Oh, I did that" or "Oh, that makes me feel good because I did that."

It truly is this life of no boasting in what I've done, because you weren't the one to put it inside you.

HE created you to be who you are with those giftings and abilities.

HE gave you the desire to develop those skills.

All your experiences were purposed by HIM.

HE has put this treasure in earthen vessels so the excellency of the power would be of HIM and not of ourselves.

So that's really what it is.

That's what it is.

10.3 A life of above and beyond

This life in HIM is above and beyond what you can ask or think.
It's only about the above and beyond.
It's a place of unlimited.
It's a place of no limits.
It's the higher place of above and beyond.
That's what this life is about.
This life is about the looking above and beyond.

Everything that you see down here is limited.
Everything down here has to be.
It can only be limited.

But in HIM there are no limits.
Everything to do with our lives in HIM is in this realm of above.
This place is the higher place.
We're born from above.
We live and move and have our being in the "being-ness" of above, although in this world.
The existence of who we are is in the above and beyond realm.
All the time.

Every time our gaze comes down, the limits start to speak and to want attention.
But that's not the truth.
The truth is, it's above and beyond.

10.4 Looking beyond

MY ways are above.

These things are higher than what you see and hear, for MY ways are higher.

My ways are of a different nature than what you see and hear.

These things will not conform or behave as things on the earth because these are things of above, and so are not of the earth.

The mind gets stuck on the things of the earth, on the earthly things seen and heard.

Look not at the earthly, but look above, at MY plan, MY purpose, and MY thoughts.

They are higher than yours.

Look up higher.

Because of these days that we're in, look beyond.

Look farther than what you see.

Look farther, beyond what you hear.

Look farther, past what you see and hear, into MY thoughts and purposes that are higher.

These are days of the above and beyond what is received in the mind.

You know this in your heart, not in your mind.

This place of looking and seeing beyond, this is the place of joy and peace.

It cannot be articulated in men's speech for it is a place in the SPIRIT where the heart rejoices.

This is the heart place where saints have gone for that drink of joy!

10.5 Moving a thought up higher

You think a thought about anything and immediately move it up higher.
You've got a thought, you move it up.
You've got a thought about anything and you move it up.
Whatever the thought is.

You are ruling and reigning through one man CHRIST JESUS, from the place where HE has seated you, because of what HE's done.
You died with HIM, so you died to the thoughts of down here.
You died to those.
A dead man has no response to things, so you're dead to the way things are down here.
You think a thought about down here, and you're dead to that thought because HE died the death with you.
You died with HIM, you're risen with HIM, and are seated with HIM above.
This new resurrection life IN HIM lifts you up out of thinking the thoughts of down here.
You think a thought about anything and you lift it up to where HIS life flows into that thought and changes and alters that thought, the very thought.
That's why HE says, "You thought it was your idea but I say it was mine."

You think a thought down here, and you think it is subject to the things that are down here, but it isn't, because it's higher.
That's why this is washing of the water by the Word because the Word just washes the thought life and moves it from down here.
In a second it has moved up to resurrection life, new life, new thought patterns, new words.

I say yes to abundant life, and no to fear and bondage.
Yes to abundant life.
It washes the thoughts from down here, and immediately it's lifted up.
That's why you get to say what HE says, because you're IN HIM, and

there's no life in anything else.

There's no power in anything else.

There's no peace in anything else.

There's no hope in anything else.

There's nothing in anything else.

It's devoid of life down here.

Only the death that HE died, and rose again, and seated us, only that could accomplish such a transformation.

That's why only the resurrection could do it, there's nothing else that could do such a profound wondrous transformation.

CHAPTER 11
Benefits of Life IN HIM

11.1 HIS extravagance

The cross demonstrated GOD's extravagant love.
GOD sending HIS only begotten SON, demonstrated HIS extravagance.
Extravagant love.
Extravagant measures.
Extravagant blood of this New Covenant to make man just like HIM.
Extravagant measures for this life.
A GOD of extravagance.
A FATHER of extravagance.
Extravagant.

Extravagant love.
Extravagant measures.
Extravagant life.
GOD making man.
Making man just like HIMSELF to make an open show to the principalities and powers and rulers of wickedness in high places.
GOD providing the LAMB.
Providing HIMSELF as the LAMB.

Extravagance of our GOD.
Extravagance in every area.
Above and beyond all that man could ask or even dream up or imagine.
Watch and see, here it comes.

11.2 Complete provision

To the Body of CHRIST:
Reason and the flesh say, "How dare you say you can live your life completely provided for?"
Reason and flesh say . . .
How dare you say that?
Who let you say that?
Who allowed you to say that?
Who gave you the right to say that?
Who gave you the right to live that way?
Who gave you that right?
You're a mere human being, subject to all the things that man is subject to.
Who gave you that right?
Who protects you?
What protects you?
What?
Who?
How?

Who?

It is CHRIST in you.
The hope of glory.
It is the reality of the glory of GOD in a human being, that's who!
This is this life.
This is this blood-bought life, the Body of CHRIST, hidden in HIM.
Hidden!

The Body of Christ talks about the devil and what he does all the time.
They fuss about the devil, when the truth is already in there.
The truth of this life is already in there.
The living of HIS resurrection life is already in there.
Already bought with the blood, even without being aware of it.
That's the truth.

11.3 Authority

You are just like ME in this world by virtue of the blood.
Not by virtue of what you think of yourself.
Not by virtue of what you know.
Not by virtue of what you feel.
Not by virtue of what you perceive.
Nor by virtue of what you've heard.
You are the righteousness of GOD in CHRIST JESUS by the authority of the blood of the New Covenant.
The authority I have given you is to be just like ME.
It is a New Covenant of the blood of JESUS.
So, this is taking your place of authority IN HIM.
There is no work of the devil that has any place in you, or has anything to say about you, because as HE is, so are you in this world.

HE took on and became a curse for you so you are free of the curse.
Free of sin.
Free of sickness.
Free of poverty.
Already free of the curse because HE became a curse so you wouldn't have to be cursed.
So your authority is backed by the "it is finished", where there's no cursing, no reception of cursing.
It is a lie of the devil that you have to accept a little bit of cursing.
A little bit here.
A little bit there.
The devil says you have to accept it.
But you've been given authority over the curse because of the blood.
You have authority, you say what happens.

The devil doesn't say what happens to you and your family.
You say what happens to you and your family.
You speak it because the blood is behind you.
The blood is backing you and enabling you.

The blood has made you free to speak to the wind and the waves.

The blood has made you free to speak to blindness and deafness.

The blood has made you free to speak to the dead to rise and be filled with life.

You are the one who has been given the authority to speak it.

You do not have to work at it or to understand working at it.

You don't have to figure it out, because it's simply seeing it and acting on it.

That's all it is.

It is simply, you are IN HIM.

You say what happens to your family.

To your money.

To your future.

You say.

You have all authority because of the blood of JESUS.

HE has given you that full authority.

You are complete in HIM.

Everything you need. Spirit. Soul. Body. You are complete in HIM.

Completely provided for.

So you speak these things as if they are done, and they are done, and that is it, and there's no fussing.

11.4 Ruling and reigning

You rule and reign because HE is in you.
Because the GREATER ONE lives in you, you rule and reign when you speak those things that are in your heart.
The truth that you know rules and reigns over the natural every time you say it.
It rules and reigns every time you speak what you know in your heart.
It rules over and it reigns over.
You rule over the natural things just as JESUS did because you are the righteousness of GOD in CHRIST.
Just as HE is, so are you in the world.

As you speak those things that you know in your heart, they actually do change material reality.
The waves stop when you speak those things you know in your heart.
The wind stops when you speak those things you know in your heart.
The blind are healed when you speak.
The deaf are healed when you speak.
The lame walk when you speak.
These things happen because you've already overcome.
Because the GREATER ONE lives in you.

The place of ruling and reigning is not what you think about yourself.
It's not what you understand about who you are.
That's not what it is.
It's not about what you understand.
It's about HIM living in you.
The GREATER ONE lives in you so you've already overcome, just like HIM.
It's already done, so just like JESUS you go to sleep in the back of the boat.
You go to sleep in the boat while the winds and the waves are moving and bringing all the fear that they do.
You go to sleep not expecting disaster and destruction.

Just like HIM you fall asleep because you know in your heart who HE is and who you are in HIM.

So you say, "Waves, you just calm down, wind you disperse, storm you leave because it's already done."

You don't have to work yourself up to rule and reign because it's already in there.

You don't have to pump yourself up to be who you already are.

11.5 Constant care

This is the place of living in HIS constant care.
Surrounded by HIS constant care.
Infused with HIS constant care.
Talk about the lilies of the field, talk about the sparrows, talk about the anything you can think of.
Talk about any single thing you can think of.
There is nothing that misses HIS gaze of constant care.
There's not the least little thing.
Not the smallest thing.
Not the most minute.
Not even the thing that takes a microscope to see.

This is a life of every single detail worked out beforehand.
The paths to walk in.
The places to go.
The people.
The circumstances.
The situations orchestrated to the minutest precision.
This is a life of the precision of the smallest element, the smallest part that is needed to complete it to perfection.

How much more your heavenly FATHER cares and watches over you and supplies every single thing.
Even the minutest thing required for life and godliness while you're here.
The smallest part and the exquisite planning of it.
The exquisite planning, and the fashioning, and the molding, and the working of it.
It is the perfecting of it in every detail.

The fashioning, the persistence of the perfecting of the fashioning.
HE, that has begun the good work in you, will perfect it until the day of JESUS CHRIST.

11.6 A new creation

GOD is at work within you both to will and to do of HIS good pleasure.
It is GOD who is at work within you.
GOD is fashioning and perfecting within you both to will and to do.
The willingness to do and the capacity to do comes from HIM.

HE is at work inside where HE dwells, to will and to do.
You are HIS workmanship and are created in CHRIST JESUS.
You are formed in HIM.
And you are created in HIM not in yourself.
It's not about you, and because it's not about you, you're not the one who decides how it looks.
HE gives you the desires of your heart.
You think you know the desires of your heart, but HE'S at work within you both to will and to do of HIS good pleasure.
HE came that you might have life and have it more abundantly.
HIS life is more abundant, full of life in every area of your life.
The truth is, HE already knows this day that you are in, because HE thought it.
It is HIS plan and HIS purpose to fashion and to give you the capacity both to will and to do.
You don't will to do, in and of yourself, but in HIM you can do all things through CHRIST who strengthens you.
Because the greater one lives in you.
Just as HE is, so are you in the world.

You are a new creation, created in CHRIST JESUS.
You take the paths which HE has preordained for you to take and walk, because HE created them for you.
HE created and destined that you would live the good life.
A life of good.
The expectation of good.
The conviction of good.
Always good.
HE is always good, and HIS work in you is for your good.

The Creator looks at HIS creation and says, "Oh, it's good, It's so good."
HE shows it to the principalities and powers and the rulers of wickedness in high places.
HE displays it openly with this blood of the New Covenant, this cross, this, "Oh, look at what I'VE accomplished, look, look. Look at it."
Look at what I'VE done.
Look at what I'VE accomplished.

It's an open show of triumph.
An open show of HIS grace.
That's why the blood is so powerful.
The blood creates and fashions.
The blood is filled with life in a new way.
It's a new creation.
The old is passed away and behold all things are now become new because of the blood of this New Covenant.
This New Covenant created in CHRIST JESUS.
Created in the CREATOR.
Created to reveal the CREATOR.
HIS creation reveals the CREATOR for everything is consummated and completed in HIM.

11.7 YOU make the way

YOU make the way.

YOU make the way, JESUS.

YOU make the way where there is no other way, because YOU are the way.

YOU are the way with the application of YOUR name to the circumstance and situation.

It's putting YOUR name on the circumstance where there is no other way.

When every sense says there's no way.

When every reasoning says there's no way.

When every sensible, reasonable, and rational reading of the circumstance says, "There is no way – give up," YOU make the way. When every sense in this realm says don't even bother, there's no way, then YOU open the way because YOU are the way.

The blood-bought ones are not regulated, controlled, enslaved to the way it is here.

Because of that, the NAME is applied to the need, and the way is released because it's already done in the heavenlies.

Whatever is already bound in the heavenlies may be bound on earth.

Whatever is already released in the heavenlies may be released on earth.

It is binding up of the lack, and the need.

And it's releasing the way for the need being met in the NAME that is above every need that can be named, on the earth.

JESUS, you are THE WAY for everything in this life.

In YOU, the blood-bought ones live.

In YOU, the blood-bought ones move, and have their being.

So, what you declare as a blood-bought one comes to pass from your heart by the application of the NAME to that circumstance.

It makes a way where there patently is no way.

So thank you LORD.

YOU do the impossible all the time.

We do not need YOU to do the possible, but the impossible.

That is the wonder of it.

That's the joy of it.

And that's the peace of it.

It's the peace that transcends our understanding on whatever the matter is.

Because whatever the matter is, it's already IN HIM.

The matter is already met, because of the application of the NAME.

The matter is already met because the blood has been shed for the whole life.

11.8 Living in the hidden place

We live in this place of "in HIM you live and move and have your being". The blood of JESUS has bought this place and paid for it, and then HE said, "It is finished."

This means everything is bought and paid for.

This means that everything that is required for life and godliness is IN HIM.

This means that everything that is required for this life is IN HIM.

This means that everything that is required for being in this life is found IN HIM.

Living and moving in this life is found IN HIM.

The mind wants to bring this into some kind of order and make it do something, but it cannot.

These things are hidden from the mind, so you cannot make order of them.

So everything is hidden IN HIM.

And everything necessary for this life comes from that hidden place.

That place where there's no fear.

That place where no fearful words have any power.

There are no words or lack of words.

There are no wrong words that can have any power in this place of the reality of JESUS.

This is the hidden place that nobody else can tap into or go to or have access to.

Everything is safe IN HIM.

The vigilance of looking all the time, and being prepared and ready, is all mind stuff.

It's trying to be ready when we can't because we're already hidden IN HIM through the blood.

It's not our readiness or our preparedness that we have to bring to this life.

It's not our ability that we have to bring to this life.

It's not anything else that we have to bring to this life.

It's actually not even the ability to say "yes" or "no" because everything is IN HIM anyway.

The "yes" or the "no" are not necessary to receive whatever HE has.

HE overrides that anyway because nothing is impossible with HIM.

This is actually the place of resting and being.

This is the place of living and moving and having our being.

This is the place of being completely subsumed in HIM.

The mind cannot grapple and explain the heart place.

The heart place is made for HIM to be in.

This is the place of life.

11.9 Always working on your behalf

I'M always working on many different fronts at the same time.
I'M always working on your behalf.
On behalf of your spirit, soul, and body.
I'M bringing things into order and into the place of "in HIM you live and move and have your being, spirit, soul, and body".
All these things work together for good for them that love GOD.
They work for good for them that are called according to HIS purpose.
So, all these things that seem to be disparate and seem to be unfinished or unresolved, I'M working on them all at once.
Spirit, soul, and body.
I'M restoring.
I'M reviving.
I'M renewing.
I'M redeeming.
I'M replenishing.
I'M doing all those things at the same time.
So really the place to be is asleep in the back of the boat.
Because the things that seem to be unresolved are actually being worked on all the time.

HE's redeeming them.
HE's renewing them, and restoring them to a new place and purpose while you rest.

Every time you try and fit into the old way it never works because it can't work.
You can't put new wine into old wineskins because they crack.
They can't hold the new wine, because the new wine is actually new life.

All this restoring and redeeming and recovering is a work of the HOLY GHOST.
In HOLY GHOST revivals God prepares people.
It is a work of the HOLY GHOST.

And this is a work of the HOLY GHOST.

It's a restoration, a recovery, a renewal, a revival, a redemption, a restoring all at the same time, spirit, soul, and body.

It seems to happen in a day although it's been happening the whole time. It's demonstrated in a day and it happens in a day, like the suddenness of it in a day.

11.10 It's already done

It's this whole business of "what do you want me to do, LORD, what do you want me to do?"
Show me what you want me to do.
How do I do this?
How do I sort this out?
What do I do?
It's this constant need to sort it out, and to do.
What do you want me to do?

And HE says, "MY thoughts are your thoughts. I am in you and you are in ME so you have the mind of CHRIST."
And HE says the mind of CHRIST gives you peace.
All that other stuff – there's no peace there!
There's never any peace about all of it.
It can only bring confusion and yet another rabbit trail.
Oh, maybe this is the way.
Oh, maybe that is the way.
Oh, maybe over here, or maybe over there.
There's no peace in it and there'll always be another rabbit trail, and it will never stop, and that's what it is.

I said I would do it on your behalf.
You don't do it.
I said I would do it on your behalf.
I've done everything.
Because it is done.
You'll see it done.
You'll see how I do it and it's done.
You'll see it demonstrated and you will walk in the done-ness of it.
You will walk in the demonstration of it.
So, you just rest and I'll do it on your behalf.
Then you just walk into it and it's done.

JESUS walked on the earth and knew the nature and character of HIS FATHER in heaven.

So, you also know the nature of your FATHER in heaven, so you know "it's already done".

JESUS was on earth in physical form but he knew the FATHER.

HE knew His nature, HE knew His character, HE knew His plan, and HE knew His purpose.

We also know our FATHER's nature which is "GOD is love, GOD is light".

As we walk here, light opens and breaks forth and love makes a way and casts out all fear.

So, as we walk these steps and these paths, that HE has for us to walk in, it's for living the good life that HE came for us to live.

It's the knowing who HE is, HIS character, HIS nature, love and light.

We walk in that all the time.

Love opens doors like Peter's miraculous deliverance from prison, and light floods the cell.

All of these things are the same because that's who HE is.

So because of HIS love, HE delivers.

Because of HIS light, HE illuminates the dark place so that it's transformed into a light-filled place where you see who He is.

A light-filled place where you know who you are.

A light-filled place where HIS love always illuminates every situation.

It's the knowledge of HIM.

It's the knowing who HE is and HIS nature and HIS being and HIS character.

HE's faithful and true, the ONE to be relied on while we're here, while HE has us here.

Every time we look at the body and the blood we're making that proclamation of HIS death and what it means, the reality of it until HE comes again.

CHAPTER 12
The Choice to Overcome Fear

12.1 The power of decision

It's about deciding.

It's about the power of decision.

You've not been given a spirit of fear but of power.

You've been given the power of decision.

You deciding, because in HIM you live and you move and you have your being.

You have the power of decision, of deciding "yes" or "no".

It isn't even about the saying, it's about the decision.

It's simply the decision.

It's simply the "yes" or the "no".

That's all it is, it's a simple decision.

Everything else actually does flow from the decision because just like HIM, so are you in this world.

So this is the power of the decision.

Decision, because fear is all around and is saying "it's not necessary," or "don't bother" for whatever reason.

Yet all it takes is the decision, because in HIM you live and you move and you have your being.

That's all it is.

It's as simple as a decision.

Fear comes in and says, "Not you, not you, you don't have to, you don't have to."

You can survive without making this decision that is filled with power, that has power, that is imbued with power.

The fear of powerlessness comes from a different spirit, a different nature.

But in HIM you've not been given a spirit of fear, but of power and love, and a sound mind.

The power of it.

The power of decision.

It's as simple as a decision.

So, it actually is Peter, looking at JESUS, and Jesus saying "come."
It's actually Peter looking at JESUS, hearing JESUS and looking at JESUS
and deciding, and taking that first step on the water.
Walking on the water with JESUS.
Seeing, and knowing,
 . . . and deciding.

12.2 Stepping out in HIM

You live and move and have your being IN HIM, so the going of it is simply putting one foot in front of another.

There's never any fear in the going.

The going does not hold fear within it.

It does not hold dread.

It does not hold doubt.

It does not hold insecurity.

It does not hold inability.

Nor does it hold wrong timing.

It's the taking of the first step, and then the second step follows.

The first step is the decision.

The first step is deciding you're going.

It's the taking of the "go, in my Name, and others will believe".

The first step is the deciding step and everything follows from that.

There is no fear or doubt or insecurity in that.

There's none of that in that first step because it's "in HIM" and in HIS name.

The deciding is looking at the first step and determining what is the first step.

How does the first step look?

What does it look like?

It's simply the taking of the first step and then everything else follows.

Everything else flows.

It's like opening the lock on a dam.

You just open it, and then everything flows from there.

It's so uncomplicated, because the first step is the only decision to be made, then everything flows.

It will be just like opening sluice gates and everything flows from that opening.

Everything flows from that, because MY thoughts are your thoughts.

12.3 The repercussions of trying to figure things out for yourself

The spirit of fear is the very nature of the symptoms and the circumstances that beset us.

The spirit of fear says, "You'd better figure me out, and if you don't figure me out there's hell to pay, so you'd better figure me out."

It just sits there and it says, "Figure me out, figure me out, figure me out, look at me, look at me, figure me out" over and over.

It can't stop because it's a spirit and it's driven.

This spirit of fear is a lust that says, "Figure me out, figure me out, or there's hell to pay."

All the reasoning and the figuring it out can't stop it though, they can only say that.

They can't say, "It is finished," because that's not the spirit that is in those words.

It can only say, "You'd better figure me out or there's hell to pay."

The blood has already dealt with the figuring it out.

For when Jesus said, "It is finished," it was finished.

That's why the figuring it out is never actually a conclusion, it's only there until the next time.

But the blood puts paid to that constant drip of it that never shuts up.

The blood shuts it down, and you are redeemed by that blood.

You are redeemed from the "figure it out, figure it out".

You are redeemed from that place, and you are bought back from the tyranny of the constant "figure it out".

Thank you, Lord.

12.4 No way out, except

Where has all the "trying to figure it out" got us?
Where has it gotten you?
All the time of figuring it out, where has it gotten you?
Around and around, and around, and around.
There's no way out through the figuring it out.
The only way out is the "Oh! It's done!"

12.5 There are no concerns

Everything in this realm, in the lower realm where you have your feet, everything comes dressed as a concern.
It comes dressed for the occasion.
It has a particular kind of appearance.
It comes dressed as a concern, a fear.
It has an outfit on that says, "You'd better be concerned, because if you're not concerned, you're foolish."
Everything in this realm that comes as a concern you'd better be concerned about.
It comes dressed in all the words and all the experience and all the reality of this lower realm.
"You'd better be concerned because if you aren't, you're foolish."

IN HIM it's the opposite for the blood-bought believer.
HE is the redeemer of "Oh! You did that wrong."
HE is the redeemer of every sickness.
HE is the redeemer of poverty in every form.
HE already took every category of concern, so you are free from the tyranny of concern.

12.6 The fear of being wrong

There's no fear in HIS love.
You've not been given a spirit of fear.
You've not been given a spirit that fears saying the wrong thing in the wrong way.
There's no fear about that.
The constant looking at what you see, with the evidence of your eyes in this realm, is filled with fear.
It's filled with fear that somebody will see it and say you're wrong.
Not just that you said the wrong thing, or did the wrong thing, but that you are inherently wrong.

That fear of a man brings a snare.
It's a trap.
It entraps you.
But you have not been given a spirit of fear of any kind of bondage.
You are not to be enslaved to how it looks or how it appears to others.
That's why this life is so demonstrably different to what you see or perceive with your senses.
It's different because you are born from above and you function from above.

Everything down here is truly subject to change.
It is subject to those Spirit declarations and proclamations from above, without any fear attached to them.
The Spirit declarations proclaim the truth that sets men free.
HE whom the SON sets free is free.
The truth sets you free.
The truth of who you are and WHOSE you are.
This is the day of the HOLY GHOST, in these vessels, in this day where there's no fear of man and no ensnarement by it.
You truly can go where you're led to go.
Do what you're led to do.
WITHOUT FEAR!

CHAPTER 13
Stop It! Just Do It!

13.1 I never told you to do it yourself

I never told you to do it yourself!
I never told you to do it yourself!
I did not equip you to do it yourself.
If I wanted you to do it yourself I would have told you and equipped you
to do it yourself.
So stop trying to do it yourself.

Lazarus was dead and buried.
He was dead and buried, there was nothing he could do.
When he heard the voice of LOVE Himself, he came alive and walked
out.
When he heard his name called by LOVE Himself, he walked out.
He had no power.
He had nothing.
He could do nothing, but at the sound, out walked the man who had been
dead.

I created you this way.
You cannot live any other way.

13.2 I don't allow it

You can disallow that thing that rises up in your life.

When it rears up its ugly head and wants a voice and a place in any part of your life, you get to say, "I don't allow it."

You get to say it because you already know it's not yours.

Say, "I don't allow it. I stop its effect, I don't allow it."

It comes from the place of "I don't expect it and I don't allow it."

So when it pops up, you say "no" and you just go on.

It's very simple and straightforward.

There's no fuss.

There's no discussion.

There's no back and forth about it.

There's no figuring it out.

No reason to question "Why is it here? What is it doing? What is it saying? How long is it going to be here?"

No, you don't even expect it.

It comes and – NO!

13.3 Why I shed my blood

So why do you think I shed my blood?
Why do you think I went to the cross?
Why do you think your heart knows what your head cannot know?
Just say NO to what your heart says NO to.
And say YES to what your heart says YES to.
So just do it!
Simple.

13.4 So stop it

Every single time you come up to anything in your life through your mind, you will fall flat on your face.

Remember, you did not choose ME for this life, but I chose you to live your life through your heart.

So every time you come up to anything through your mind, you will fall flat on your face.

So stop it!

13.5 Expulsion

The symptoms and earthly things that beset us are like naughty children in a schoolhouse.

The naughty children in a schoolhouse continue to manifest their presence despite our "dealing with them".

They like their naughtiness to be shown off in front of the class, and they revel in being allowed to continue their naughtiness.

Every morning the schoolmarm admonishes them, and scolds them, and warns them, and they thrive on the recognition.

Every day the process is repeated and the naughty children giggle and nudge one another and try to look embarrassed.

They promise to reform, and every day the process is repeated.

The only solution is to expel the naughty children.

The teacher has as much authority to expel them as she does to scold them.

But she has resisted doing so until she comes to the place of recognition and understanding of her authority.

Until she comes to the place of recognition of the final and absolute need for an end to the problem.

Expulsion!

13.6 Let it go, it's just baggage

Let it go.
Just let it go.
It doesn't hurt, whatever your "it" is, let it go.
You're not diminished.
Let it go.
You're not less than.
Let it go.
If you want to carry it, if you want to hold it to yourself, add it to who you are, you are free to.
But just let it go.
It's just baggage.
So, let it go.
It does not add to you.
It does not speak of you.
It does not demonstrate who you are because you are in HIM, and you live and move and have your being in HIM.
Everything else is to be let go.
You don't have to carry it.
You can carry it if you want to.
You can carry it on your back like a heavy sack, but you don't have to.
It's your choice, so just let it go.

HE said, "MY yoke is easy and MY burden is light," so you don't have to carry anything else.
You don't have to carry anything that is heavy or constricting or difficult.
You just let it go because HIS yoke is easy.
It's easy.
This fused relationship with HIM is easy.
It's not hard, and difficult, and heavy, and burdensome, and onerous, and ponderous, and all those other words.
Just ease and peace.
MY burden is easy.
MY yoke is easy.

MY burden is easy, easy, easy.

It's just in HIM and so there's no heavy, difficult, or onerous problem.

It's easy being who you are already in JESUS, because of the blood, HIS life in you.

So just as HE is, so are you in this world.

13.7 Just because you don't see it . . .

Just because you don't see or hear or perceive of what I'm doing, and how I do it, just because you don't perceive it, doesn't mean that I'm not doing it.

Did I not tell you that if you believe, you will receive.
Whatever you ask the FATHER in MY Name, HE will do it.
HE will do it.
That is HIS word about what HE does in your life in this realm.

Just because you don't see it yet, or perceive it, or feel it in your senses, does not mean that HE is not working on your behalf in every situation to bring what you asked.

Because His word never fails.
Never!

CHAPTER 14
The Power of Words

14.1 Your words and my life

The reality is that it's not the accuracy of the words that you speak, but it is MY power and life that is in the words.

It is MY power that is the agent of change through the words you speak.

It is not the accuracy of the words, those are mere clothing.

They're merely a covering, a clothing, on MY Spirit in the words.

So you speak words that you understand but I release MY power, and MY ability, and MY life.

I release MY power, and MY ability, and MY life into that situation through the vehicle of the words.

The words themselves are merely forms, but the power within the words is MY life.

It's ME that goes straight to the circumstance, and changes the things that are not into what I have determined them to be.

So you speak those things that are not as though they were.

You speak them in words that you understand, but I use your voice, your breath, to activate MY plan and purpose for that situation.

It goes and does the work.

It's filled with power, MY power, MY ability, and MY Spirit, because it's not by your might or power, but by MY SPIRIT, says the LORD.

I do the work in that situation, clothed in words that you understand.

This way you have some recognition of your participation in the process of releasing SPIRIT life into that situation.

Where resurrection life goes and brings life to a situation that otherwise is dead.

Therefore you say to those things which are not.

You call them into being as though they were.

The things which are not, which have no life, you call life into them to demonstrate who I am and who you are.

14.2 Power of words

HE has made you HIS righteousness in GOD, in CHRIST JESUS, so that as HE is so are you in the world.

You died with HIM.

You rose with HIM.

You are seated with HIM, so that you are as HE is in the world.

There is power in your words that are spoken from that place of permanence where there's no change.

That place where there's no shadow of another agenda hidden in words.

When you speak those words from the heart, then there is power in your words.

When you speak from that place of being seated with him, then there is power in your words.

When your heart knows things your head does not know, then there is power in your words.

Because of that, the things that are subject to change, do change according to the words, filled with HIS life, that are spoken.

They are changed by the words emanating and originating from light because GOD is light and GOD is love and HE is resident in you.

HE is in union and communion with you, where love is brought to completion.

Because of that, the words that are spoken from that place have inherent power.

Those words resident within are filled with the life of GOD inside.

They are HIS breath coming out.

They speak light into darkness, where darkness is transformed into light.

They speak love into condemnation.

You speak from love where there's no fear of rejection, or shame, or distance from HIM.

So, you truly are as HE is in this world, speaking light and love into situations that are, by their nature, dark and filled with fear of shame, accusation, guilt, and distance from FATHER, SON, and HOLY SPIRIT.

Love came in and changed things, making this life new, one with HIM, FATHER, SON, and HOLY SPIRIT.

Just as they are one, so we are one, IN HIM.

We are one, where there's no darkness and no distance from HIM.

It's all accomplished because of the blood and the body in this New Covenant.

Because of this new creation, this new being, everything changes when you speak those words.

Even as a little child responds to affirmation, so in the atmosphere of those words, people respond to the power of love in those words.

They rise to it and they start to see themselves through that love and the light of those words.

14.3 Stepping out on HIS words

The declaring and proclaiming of what's in the heart sweeps away the morass of details.

It's not about the little details.

It's not about the details of the day.

It's about the simplicity of saying "the LORD will supply," and it sweeps everything else out of the way.

The statement, the stating of it, and the proclaiming of what's in the heart, actually sweeps the morass of details.

They get swept into the force of that word from the heart.

Everything gets swept into the force of that where every detail that's needed for "the LORD will supply", is supplied.

Everything gets swept into those words.

HIS words, declared through our mouths, sweep everything.

HIS words that we speak have the force to attract and to sweep everything else into agreement with those words.

14.4 You get to say what you want

You get to say what you want!

YOU get to say what YOU want!

YOU get to SAY what you want!

YOU get to say it.

Somebody else doesn't get to say it on your behalf, YOU get to say it.

You're the one bought with the Blood.

You're the one made the righteousness of CHRIST.

You're the one died with HIM, risen with HIM, with HIS authority and HIS name.

You get to say what you want, and the supply comes and runs to your words, just like iron filings to a magnet.

Then every other obstacle is swept away.

This calling and gifting on your lives is specific and unique and has never been before.

It will not be repeated because it's specific to you and who HE made you to be.

So, that you can speak to things which wouldn't matter to anyone else.

You can speak to those things, "Come to me in JESUS' Name," "Go in Jesus' Name."

You can speak "yes" or "no".

You can do the speaking and all the supernatural comes rushing in to the natural at the sound of the words.

The supply comes to those words.

The supply rushes to those words.

14.5 Declare what you know to be true

You declare out of your own mouth what you know to be true.
Out of your own mouth, you declare what you know to be true.
The BODY and the BLOOD.
TRUE!
The WORD, made flesh, dwelt among us.
TRUE!
We behold HIS glory.
The glory of the only begotten SON of the FATHER, full of grace and truth.
TRUE!
You died with HIM, you died to all the "down here".
TRUE!
HE became the curse, and rose without it, you rose in HIM without the curse.
TRUE!
You are seated in heavenly places in Christ.
TRUE!
So you get to say what you know to be true.
You get to declare what you know to be true.

CHAPTER 15
The Blood

15.1 The Blood never stops

So you think you know these things.

You think you already know these things, and you do.

You do know these things in your heart.

I keep on telling you every second you're alive that it never stops because the blood never stops.

The life is in the blood, and MY blood was shed and given to you as this life where it's continuous.

It never stops.

The Blood never stops because it continues to speak of MY life.

The Blood continues to speak of resurrection life, and so it will never stop. It will always be, "Try it now, try it now, try it now. Whatever the circumstance, whatever the thought, just try it now."

It never stops, so I'll say the same thing again, and again, and again because it's MY life inside your body.

It's MY life that is at work quickening your mortal body, as long as you're here.

Quickening.

Restoring.

Renewing.

Redeeming.

The blood is eternal and it never stops.

The message is the same and I will keep on saying it however you need it, every moment of every day that you're here.

Because it's eternal!

In this realm, you think you have this sewn up, "I know what this is, and it's in a little box with a ribbon on it and I put it on the shelf."

And you say you know that and that's finished, but in ME the flow never stops.

But it's actually life inside your body going all the time, renewing, restoring, and redeeming.

It's always cleansing your thoughts from being down here.

It's a continuous washing of the water by the Word and it'll never stop as long as you're here, and you need it.

It's there because it's life inside your body, washing and washing and washing, because it's needed down here, so it never stops.

The simplicity of the covering power of the blood never stops with every breath that you take, with every thought that you think.

It's as simple as, "I've got you covered because of the blood."

It's eternal and it's working inside your physical vessel every moment.

15.2 The protection of the blood

From the foundation of the world I made you to be carried.
You are MY treasure.
You are the treasure of MY love.
I carry MY treasure.
The plan for MY treasure is mine.
No one touches MY treasure, this treasure in earthen vessels.
You are MINE bought with MY Blood.
I carry you through every day that you are here.
No one can snatch you from ME.
You are redeemed and protected by MY Blood.
In these days of such turmoil, MY treasure is kept because you are MINE.
These days outside are one thing, but in ME you live and you move.
You are my treasure, made just for me.
The attacks have no impact on MY treasure.
They cannot get through the Blood.
I am unveiling the power of the Nlood that repels the attacks.
It has everything to do with "bought by the Blood".
You are MY treasure.

15.3 Living the impossible life

The Blood is always flowing.

It flows up to the highest mountain and it flows down to the lowest valley. The Blood is always moving towards whatever the need is and to whatever the circumstance is.

The Blood is always flowing because it's already accomplished in the heavens.

In this realm, and in the interface between the two realms, the blood is always flowing. It's this connector.

It's like a connector between the two realms, and it's always efficacious.

It's always filled with power and the reality of "it is finished", over, and over, and over again.

It's like that washing of the water by the WORD.

It continuously washes the thoughts and cleanses the thoughts.

It cleanses always, constantly.

It cleanses the thoughts of the dust of down here, and the dirt of down here, and the fear of down here.

This continual process and continual washing always says, "I've got it covered, I have it covered."

It always says, "It's already accomplished. You just rest and let ME do the doing."

You just rest in that efficacious, redeeming power of the blood that never loses any power.

It's never diminished. It's never lost. It's never changed.

This is the power of the Blood of the New Covenant that says, "It is finished."

Cast every concern and every care on HIM because this Blood is the Blood of "I have it covered".

Don't give it a care because HE already cared for it and has already taken it.

Whatever is a care for you, HE's already taken and paid for the care to be resolved and accomplished.

Your part is simply to rest in HIM.

Rest in the drowning out of taking the care yourself.

Rest and allow HIS "I have done it" to override and to drown out the "Oh, what about this, and what about that?"

It's allowing HIS "I have it covered" to override and to overwhelm the constant drip of "you have to be the solution to this, whatever the 'this' is". Thank you, Lord. YOU have it covered and that's it.

So, we live this impossible life, this absolutely impossible life that we're not meant to live on our own, because we can't.

It's not designed to be lived by ourselves, on our own power, in our own ability, because it's an impossible life, by design.

We are created as new creatures in CHRIST JESUS. New creatures and that's it.

That's what this life is. Created so you can't do it.

So that's it!

15.4 The work of the Blood in the believer

When we praise HIM and sing about the freedom of the blood, there is an anointing and a quickening, and yokes are destroyed.
The yokes and the constrictions are moved out of the way.
The struggles and the troubles are moved out of the way.
The rocks that are in the way are moved out of the way.
The rocks and the rubble are pushed out of the way by the flow of HIS life Blood.
It's the business of stepping onto the water in the SPIRIT.
By and through and in the SPIRIT.
Stepping out onto the water and into the things of the SPIRIT.
It's being and moving in that place in the SPIRIT.
It's actually prepared inside you, and you are stepping out on to the water where there's no visible means of support.
It's already prepared for you so it's just "Oh! OK", that's all it is, it's not anything else.
It's not any big horrendous, momentous decision, it's simply "Oh! OK".
That's all this is in the SPIRIT realm.

It's simple.
It's not complicated.
It's not fraught with "what about?", and "how do I?", and "what do I?", and "when do I?".
It's simply "Oh! OK", and that's all it is because it's simply who you are.
It's how you move and how you have your being.
So it is simple.

It's not an onerous thing and there are no qualifications for it except the Blood.
It's only being washed in the Blood.
It is so simple because it's hidden from the mind, because the mind has nothing to say about these things in the SPIRIT.
The mind of the flesh wants to sort things out.
The mind of the flesh wants to manage it and control it and teach a course on it and all that stuff.

The mind wants to know how to do in the SPIRIT, or how to be in Him, but it has nothing to say.

Those things do not submit to the things of GOD, because they can't and they won't.

They won't be put into a little box that's labeled "this is how you do it", because it's by the SPIRIT of the LORD.

It's in the SPIRIT and it's through the SPIRIT.

It's simply living and moving and having your being in the SPIRIT.

That's all it is.

The mind trips over those things and makes it hard work.

Of course, it's hard work because it's not done in the mind.

So the mind can't do it.

The mind can't function in the SPIRIT.

It can't sort out how to do it, what steps to take to do this, because there's no accessing it by the mind.

So this "in HIM you live and move and have your being" has no reference point to somebody else because it's In HIM.

The blood has bought this place for the believer.

The continual referencing and looking at one another has no power in it.

There's no freedom in it.

There's no place in it.

There's no anointing in it.

There's no anointing in the looking at one another.

That's not the reality of "in HIM you live, and you move, and you have your being IN HIM".

So, every single time in this lower level you look at someone else you are powerless.

There's no power in that.

It's all behavioral and external, because it doesn't come from the place of "in HIM you live, and you have your being".

Intrinsically you are in HIM and joined to HIM

He who is joined to the LORD is one SPIRIT with HIM.

As FATHER and SON and SPIRIT are one, so you are joined in that triumvirate.

You are not in the looking at the times past.
You're not in the looking at what went before.
You're not in all the looking.
You're not in all the figuring out.
You're not in all the trying to retrace steps.
You're not in all the looking to all the wonderful moves of GOD that have gone before.
You're not in those moves.
You are in HIM.

You are joined to HIM in whom you live and move and have your being.
You're not joined to those "before places".
That was for then and this is for now.
Just like Peter with the sheet, there was a time for that and this is the time for now.

So it is actually altogether different.
It will not look like what has gone before.
It will not conform to what has gone before.

15.5 New Covenant existence

So, this New Covenant life, this life of the blood of the New Covenant, cannot be lived in old covenant fashion, in an old covenant way.
It cannot be lived that way.
It is impossible.
It can't be done, however one tries to obey through demand.

Trying to be worthy.
Trying to do enough.
It will never be enough.
It cannot be enough to access the things that the blood of the New Covenant has bought and paid for.
It will never work because it is not designed to work.
It was only designed to show the bankruptcy of demand.
To show the bankruptcy of living through the achievement of the flesh.

This new wine cannot be put in old wineskins, because it bursts the container.
That's why this new life, this resurrection life, can only be received by the blood-washed.
It can only be received by the blood-redeemed and the blood-bought receptacle.
It's the only receptacle that can receive what the blood of the New Covenant has accomplished.
The blood of the cross says everything is finished because JESUS accomplished everything.
Because of JESUS, there is nothing left to be accomplished.
There is only the receiving of what has already been accomplished.

Any time the blood-bought ones endeavour to achieve God's blessing, it comes to nothing because there's no life in it.
There's no help in personal endeavour.
There's no life in it.

That's why this walk and this being, this blood-bought new creation, this being in HIM, never conforms to any kind of achievement. Any achievement carries with it a tension to the one who achieved it.

So any time a blood-bought one tries to achieve, it's empty.

There's nothing in it.

It falls to the ground like dead leaves.

The attention is all to JESUS, the ONE who shed the blood, not the one who is bought by the blood.

So it is altogether different.

This work of the blood.

So that's our place in this blood-bought, New Covenant existence.